08
£6·60

People and Power in the Pacific

The Struggle for the Post-Cold War Order

WITHDRAWN FROM THE
FCO LIBRARY

Walden Bello

Foreword by Ted Wheelwright

D1585474

FOREIGN & COMMONWEALTH OFFICE LIBRARY

Pluto Press

with *Food First,*

and Transnational Institute (TNI)

London • San Francisco

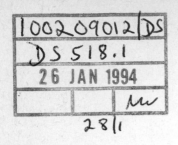

100209012/DS
DS 518.1
26 JAN 1994
ℳ
28/1

First published 1992 by Pluto Press
345 Archway Road, London N6 5AA
in association with the
Institute for Food and Development Policy (*Food First*),
145 Ninth Street, San Francisco, CA 94103, USA;
and with the Transnational Institute (TNI),
Paulus Potterstraat 20, 1071 DA, Amsterdam

Distributed in the Netherlands by
the Transnational Institute

Copyright © Walden Bello 1992

The right of Walden Bello to be identified as author of this work has been
asserted by him in accordance with the Copyright, Designs and Patent Act
1988.

British Library Cataloguing in Publication Data
A catalogue record for this book is available from the British Library

ISBN 0 7453 0697 7 (hb)
ISBN 0 7453 0698 5 (pb)

Library of Congress Cataloging in Publication Data
Bello. Walden F.
  People and power in the Pacific : the struggle for the post-Cold
War order / Walden Bello : foreword by Ted Wheelwright.
  152p. 22cm. – (Transnational Institute series)
  Simultaneously published by the Institute for Food and Development
Policy (Food First) and Pluto Press without the series statement.
  Includes bibliographical references and index.
  ISBN 0-7453-0697-7 (hbk) – ISBN 0-935028-60-9 (pbk.)
  1. East Asia–Politics and government. 2. Asia, Southeastern-
-Politics and government–1945- 3. East Asia–Economic conditions.
4. Asia, Southeastern–Economic conditions. 5. East Asia-
-Relations–United States. 6. United States–Relations–East Asia.
7. Asia, Southeastern–Relations–United States. 8. United States-
-Relations–Asia, Southeastern. I. Title. II. Series.
DS518.1.B45   1992b
947–dc20   92-29810
                                                                        CIP

Food First paperback edition (US only)
ISBN 0–935028–60–9

Typeset by Stanford Desktop Publishing Services, Milton Keynes
Printed and bound in the United States of America

WITHDRAWN FROM TH'
FCU LIBRARY

About the Author

Dr Walden Bello is the executive director of the Institute for Food and Development Policy (*Food First*) in San Francisco. He is a native of Manila, the Philippines, and obtained his PhD in political sociology from Princeton University.

Dr Bello's publications include *Development Debacle: The World Bank in the Philippines* (Food First, 1982); *American Lake: Nuclear Peril in the Pacific* (Penguin, 1987, co-authored with Peter Hayes and Lyuba Zarsky); *Visions of a Warless World* (Friends Committee on National Legislation, Washington DC, 1987); *Brave New Third World: Strategies for Survival in the Global Economy* (Earthscan, 1990); *Dragons in Distress: Asia's Miracle Economies in Crisis* (Penguin, 1991, co-authored with Stephanie Rosenfeld), and numerous journal articles.

He is currently contributing editor for Pacific News Service, and research associate for the Center on South East Asian Studies.

Ted Wheelwright

Until his recent retirement Ted Wheelwright was associate professor of economics at the University of Sydney. He is a distinguished expert on the Australian and Chinese economies, and is currently vice-president of the Evatt Foundation.

Food First

Food First or the Institute for Food and Development Policy is a non-profit research and educational center based in San Francisco, USA, and Manila, Philippines. Founded in 1975 by Frances Moore Lappe and Joe Collins, Food First is dedicated to uncovering the genuine causes of world hunger, poverty and inequality. It also seeks to contribute to the search for strategies of development that are ecologically sustainable, equitable and democratic.

To Ami, Annette and Tonette –
warm companions, true friends

Contents

WITHDRAWN FROM TH
FCO LIBRARY

Tables, Maps and Figures

Tables

Maps and Figures

Abbreviations

ANZUS	Australia-New Zealand-United States Mutual Defense Treaty Organization
APEC	Asia-Pacific Economic Cooperation
ASEAN	Association of Southeast Asian Nations
CSCE	Conference on Security and Cooperation in Europe
DCP	Defense Cooperation Program (South Pacific)
EAEG	East Asia Economic Group
EEZ	Exclusive Economic Zone
EOI	Export-oriented Industrialization
EPZ	Export Processing Zone
FBIS	Foreign Broadcast Information Service
FLNKS	*Front de libération kanak et socialiste* (New Caledonia)
IRRI	International Rice Research Institute
JACADS	Johnston Island Chemical Disposal System
JATAN	Japan Tropical Action Network
JDA	Japan Defense Agency
KCIA	Korean Central Intelligence Agency
LDP	Liberal Democratic Party (Japan)
NDF	National Democratic Front (Philippines)
NGO	Non-governmental Organization
NIC	Newly Industrializing Country
NPA	New People's Army (Philippines)
OEM	Original Equipment Manufacture
SEATO	Southeast Asia Treaty Organization
SPNFZ	South Pacific Nuclear Free Zone
UNCLOS	United Nations Convention on the Law of the Sea

Note: 1 billion = 1000000000
Currency is US$ unless indicated otherwise

Acknowledgements

Preparing this book was an extremely gratifying experience at the personal as well as the institutional level. I am especially indebted to the following colleagues and friends: Eric Blantz of the Institute for Food and Development Policy; Joel Rocamora and Dan Smith of the Transnational Institute; Bob Debus of the Australian Freedom from Hunger Campaign; Vicky Berry and Erlinda Senturias of the Commission on International Affairs of the World Council of Churches; and Ruth Duba and the Committee on Social Witness Policy of the Presbyterian Church (USA).

I am also grateful for the stimulating intellectual companionship on Asia-Pacific issues provided over the years by Peter Hayes, Lyuba Zarsky, Julia Estrella, Marybeth Brangen, Jim Heddle, Glen Alcalay and Victor Hsu. My colleagues at the Institute for Food and Development Policy – Marilyn Borchardt, John Gershman, Stephanie Rosenfeld, Martha Katigbak, Denise Newman and Sanae Miyaji – tolerated my numerous lapses from administrative duties in the course of finishing this project, and for this I am grateful. And for that dose of camaraderie necessary to preserve one's sanity in the most trying of times, I am grateful to my wife Marilen, Amihan, Annette, Tonette Garcia and Boying Pimentel.

Roger van Zwanenberg, Linda Etchart and Toni Bird were generous with their skills, time and advice in the production of this book. I would like to express my gratitude to them and to those organizations that provided financial support for the preparation of different sections of this work: Evatt Foundation, Australian Freedom from Hunger Campaign, World Council of Churches, Presbyterian Church (US), Pohaku Fund, H.C. Gemmer Family Christian Foundation, and the Max and Anna Levinson Foundation. Though generous with their support, these institutions are not to be held responsible for the views expressed in this study or for any errors of fact and analysis that it may contain. I alone assume responsibility for this report.

Walden Bello
San Francisco
July 1992

Foreword

Ted Wheelwright

This is an incisive, powerful and prescient book.

It begins by discussing the different dimensions of the US impact on the Asia-Pacific, with the aim of understanding the constraints and opportunities afforded by this legacy in the future development of the region.

It is argued that the US presence has been mainly military in nature. The origins and consequences of this expansion are analyzed, including the political consequences that accompanied American hegemony; the social impact and environmental consequences of US-promoted patterns of development; and the 'strategic colonialism' practised by the US and its allies.

The second part of this book is equally insightful and provocative. It focuses on the rise of Japan as the main economic power in the region; the integration of the economies of Southeast Asia, including Australia, into the Japanese economic sphere of influence; and the disturbing implications of the rising antagonism between Japan and the United States.

The last section presents the vision of an alternative regional order. The key elements of this order would be an alternative security system and an alternative regional economy which would promote more regional independence, greater equity and a better environment. Especially deserving of attention is the proposal for a regional congress of non-governmental organizations that would promote the protection of human, social and environmental rights in a new Asia-Pacific order.

The sponsors of the research on which this path-breaking book is based should be proud of the final product, for not only does it accurately describe and analyze political and economic trends but it convincingly argues for an alternative Pacific future based on the extension of the concept of individual rights to society and the physical environment.

Ted Wheelwright
Vice-President, Evatt Foundation
Sydney, August 1992

Part I
America's Pacific

1
The End of the Cold War in the Pacific

In 1991, the Asia-Pacific region began to adjust, dramatically, to the end of the Cold War, much to the dismay of the United States, long the premier power in the region.

Malaysia's prime minister Mahathir Mohamed administered the first shock when he proposed the establishment of an 'East Asia Economic Group' (EAEG) that would exclude the United States and be led by Japan. So alarmed were US officials that Secretary of State James Baker journeyed to Seoul in November to warn members of the Asia-Pacific Economic Cooperation Council that 'We can never approve this regionalism which is designed to split the Asian-Pacific region and divide Japan and the United States.'[1]

Events in the Philippines delivered the second jolt. A volcanic explosion forced the US to close down Clark Air Force Base. But far more consequential was the Philippine Senate's rejection of the 'Treaty of Friendship, Cooperation, and Security' that would have extended the stay of the 91-year-old naval base at Subic Bay. Long accustomed to thinking of Filipinos as 'little brown Americans', Washington found it difficult to accept Senate president Jovito Salonga's ringing declaration that 'Today we have summoned the political will to stand up and end 470 years of foreign military presence in the Philippines.'[2]

With the cohesion provided by the Cold War disappearing, the definition of both the national interest and the regional interest began to be extricated from the narrow parameters to which it had been confined for more than 40 years by anti-communist ideology. Indeed, the two initiatives were informed by dynamic visions of a new regional order: while Mahathir sought to lay the groundwork for an Asia-Pacific bloc competing in equal terms with the emerging 'North American Free Trade Area' and the single European market in a world divided by regional blocs, the Philippine anti-bases movement saw itself as part of a broader regional effort to denuclearize and demilitarize the Asia-Pacific.

The debate posed two of the central issues in the search for a post-Cold War order: the future of the United States and the role of

Japan. Even as the region became more ambivalent about the US military presence, it also became more wary of Japan's economic strength. While most governments supported Mahathir's demand for more regional autonomy from the United States, few were willing to follow the Malaysian prime minister, widely reputed as a Japanophile, in his endorsement of Japanese leadership of the region.

Moreover, there was greater awareness that the increasingly volatile relationship between the two countries would greatly affect the future of the whole region. While official rhetoric in Washington and Tokyo continued to affirm the 'complementary relationship' of American military strength and Japanese technoeconomic power, it was obvious to everyone that the old alliance was dissolving in antagonism. President George Bush's visit to Japan in January 1992, which was upstaged by the bitter wrangling between Japanese car manufacturers and the chiefs of the US automobile industry that accompanied him, merely confirmed this reality for Asians. And they were fearful of the likely prospect that their region would become the prime area of contention between the ageing superpower and the rising challenger.

Australians had their particular apprehensions over the unravelling US–Japan relationship. Looking to the US for political leadership but dependent on Japan economically, Australians felt that their traditional degree of maneuver would be lost in any regional arrangement that was not based on a partnership between the US and Japan. Already, they felt threatened by Mahathir's EAEG concept, for it would exclude not only the US but also Australia from an Asia-Pacific economic bloc.

For most countries in the Asia-Pacific region, however, the US–Japan conflict spelled not simply peril but promise. Promise because contention between the two powers provided the smaller nations with opportunities and space to maneuver in their effort to push a truly regional agenda. Peril because, unless checked, the conflict could develop dynamics similar to the ones that led to the outbreak of the Second World War.

The rest of this decade thus offers a window of opportunity for ushering in an era marked by less conflict, less domination and less poverty and inequality. That window, however, is precariously poised and can be unhinged at any moment by the winds of change.

This report is divided into three parts. The first investigates the different dimensions of the US impact on the region, with the aim of understanding the constraints and opportunities afforded by this legacy for the future development of the Asia-Pacific. The American presence in the region has been principally of a military nature, and the mainsprings, dynamics, reach and consequences of US military expansion are examined. The mechanisms of political influence that accompanied American military hegemony are briefly discussed, followed by an extended analysis of the social impact and environmental consequences of the pattern of economic development promoted by the US. This section concludes with an examination of the persistence of the practice of strategic colonialism in the South Pacific by the US and its allies France and Indonesia, and of the roles played by Australia and New Zealand in the region.

The second part of this report focuses on the rise of Japan as the region's premier economic power, the integration of the Asia-Pacific economies around the needs of the Japanese economy, and the rising antagonism between the US and Japan. This clash is likely to supplant the Cold War as the main conflict in the Asia-Pacific in the next decade.

With the aim of 'containing' the US–Japan antagonism and other potential regional conflicts, the final section offers an alternative security framework for the region. This is followed by a proposal for an alternative economic order that would promote an economic development process that enhances regional independence, equity and environmental wellbeing. The report concludes by proposing the establishment of a 'regional congress of NGOs' (non-governmental organizations) that would ensure the protection of human, social and environmental rights in a transformed Asia-Pacific. In terms of scope, this report does not cover South Asia, Southwest Asia and the Middle East.

2

America's Contradictory Legacy

One of the questions that is uppermost in the Pacific today is the future of US power in the region.

It is a question that was unthinkable just a few years ago when both friend and foe regarded the Pacific as an 'American Lake'. As long as the Cold War was in place, America's pervasive military might was accepted as a fact of life by most governments in the region. The system of 'forward defense' was seen as providing a shield behind which not only American corporations could profit but the whole region could prosper. In the 1960s and 1970s, Herman Kahn and other American technocratic optimists foresaw a century of Pacific prosperity marked by ever tighter integration between the region's economies and the US economy.

The 1980s, however, ushered in a situation that was decidedly different in many respects from this optimistic scenario. The Asia-Pacific indeed became the world's prime growth area, but it was a development that benefited mainly the Japanese economy. The dream of trans-Pacific prosperity increasingly gave way to trade wars that pitted the US against not only Japan but also South Korea and Taiwan. The end of the Cold War sparked long-repressed challenges to the massive US military presence, which was also under attack from the so-called 'new isolationists' who saw it as one of the millstones dragging down the US economy. Indeed, from the new frontier that promised limitless expansion for US business, the Asia-Pacific has been transformed in the American consciousness into a threat to the 'American way of life'.

The contours of the future place of the United States in the Asia-Pacific is unclear. But what is clear in the 140 years since Commodore Matthew Perry opened up Japan to western trade is that the US presence has profoundly reshaped the region, for better or for worse. It is a legacy that evokes ambivalent, indeed, contradictory feelings among people throughout the region, and among not a few Americans.

America's anti-colonial heritage is one that has inspired many leaders of independence movements in the region, not the least of them being the Vietnamese Ho Chi Minh, who invoked Thomas

Jefferson's 'All men are created equal' in declaring his country's freedom from the French in August 1945. Yet it was also in the Asia-Pacific, with the onset of the Cold War in the late 1940s, that Washington launched its first experiments in neocolonial control – the sponsorship of formally independent but subservient regimes that could be counted on to promote US strategic and economic interests. And nearly three decades after the decade of decolonization in the 1960s, Washington has just consummated a classical colonial act: transforming the islands making up the United Nations Trust Territory of the Pacific into commonwealths or 'freely associated states' of the United States.

The ideology of democracy, with its emphasis on the principles of individual choice, popular government and majority rule, was another American 'export' that found wide resonance in the region. Yet, in country after country, democratic movements were sacrificed by US policymakers who chose to back dictators like Ferdinand Marcos or feudal despots like Ngo Dinh Diem in the interest of 'national security'. Moreover, in those countries where democratic politics appears to be more solidly rooted, like the Philippines, the process is most often a caricature of democratic governance, with electoral competition being essentially a contest among different factions of a wealthy elite for the privilege of ruling millions of people trapped in an extremely anti-democratic economic and social structure.

The US is also credited with stimulating the economic development of the region, with the magnet of its market (the world's biggest), the investments of its corporations, and its generous aid programs. Yet, whether in Korea, Thailand or the Philippines, the growth in the GNP that came with export-oriented development was accompanied by worsening distribution of income; and by political repression, as governments seeking American and foreign investors imposed labor policies banning trade unionism and assuring a supply of cheap labor. Moreover, from Seoul to Bangkok, export-oriented, high-speed growth in the American model has created a profound ecological crisis as forests are leveled by the buzzsaw and the bulldozer, rivers are rendered biologically dead by industrial wastes, and cities are cloaked with smog worse than Los Angeles's.

But perhaps Americans are most gratified when they hear Asians praise them for 'holding the line' and saving the region from communism, with its repressive political practice and its ineffective economics. But for every Asian who feels this way, there is likely to be one who sees things differently, who recalls that in the struggle against communism, the US literally destroyed societies in order to save them, leaving behind a legacy of fraternal hatred and, in the case of Korea, a divided nation. Moreover, wars that were justified as crusades against Soviet communism turned out to be struggles against anti-colonial movements that were more nationalist than communist and behaved just as independently toward Moscow as they did toward Washington. Thus the question is posed: would not China, North Korea and Vietnam have become part of the Asia-Pacific community more rapidly and less painfully had the US accommodated their governments as anti-colonial, nationalist forces rather than seeking to destroy them as agents of Soviet communism?

One hundred and forty years of interaction with the United States have, indeed, transformed the face of the Asia-Pacific region. For some, that transformation has been largely benign, a process represented by the spread of the democratic ideal and economic growth. But for other Asian and Pacific peoples, domination is the essence of the American presence, and the US continues to behave today in much the same fashion as in the early 1850s, when it forced Japan to open up to American trade.

Though on the decline, the US remains a formidable presence in the region, and it shows no sign of 'going gently into that good night', to borrow a line from Dylan Thomas. The US and the Pacific are on the threshold of a new century, but the hand of the past lies heavy on their future relationship. Understanding the mainsprings and complex dynamics of the US expansion and hegemony in the region is the first step in any attempt to transform that relationship.

3

The Rise of a Pacific Power

The 'Black Ships' Arrive

'We cannot sleep at night for terror and admiration of the black ships.'[1] Thus did a Japanese poet describe the state of mind of Tokyo's population at the arrival of Commodore Matthew Perry's flotilla of 'black ships' in Tokyo Bay in 1853. Perry's mission was unequivocal: open Japan to trade, by force if necessary. His success was to establish the US as a major player in the Pacific, at the same level as Britain and the other European powers, which were at this time also forcing neighboring China to accede to unequal treaties.

It was not unusual that it took a naval officer rather than a merchant to open Japan to American commerce, for in America's century-long drive to the western Pacific, trade followed the flag more frequently than the flag followed trade. At the time the US made its next major move in the western Pacific – its 8000 mile leap to the Philippines in 1898 – less than 10 per cent of US trade crossed the Pacific, while 60 per cent crossed the Atlantic. China, Korea and Japan were sources of exotic imports rather than export markets. And investments in the region were negligible; indeed, 'American capital for the exploitation of China [was] being raised with difficulty.'[2]

What lay behind the great leap westward was not a business cabal but a 'strategic lobby' of naval and political expansionists who were mainly interested in extending the reach of the US state. Entrepreneurs operating in Hawaii, the Philippines, China and the interstices of the dominant European empires vociferously supported the expansion, but they did not constitute the center of gravity of US business. That center was in New York, which was oriented far more towards Europe than Asia. Like the American missionaries who saw China as a massive opportunity for saving souls for Protestant Christianity, which was impeded by hopeless corruption in Europe and by Roman Catholicism in Latin America, business interests played an important but secondary role.

The US Navy, in particular, became particularly adept at invoking commercial rationale to promote US strategic extension, and thus its own role as the cutting edge of that mission. Acquiring bases in the far reaches of the Pacific would, among other things, provide a powerful impetus to the creation of a 'two-ocean' navy, which would be necessary to achieve the goal of 'maritime supremacy' envisioned by the fleet's leading strategic thinker, Captain Alfred Mahan.

Led by the influential Mahan and Assistant Secretary of the Navy Theodore Roosevelt, the US Navy was the main force behind the acquisition of Hawaii, Guam and the Philippines, following Admiral George Dewey's victory over the Spanish squadron in Manila Bay in May 1898. The small island of Guam in the Marianas and the Philippine archipelago were depicted as stepping stones to the riches of China to justify their annexation in the face of great opposition in the US, but Washington's main desire was Guam and the Philippines' strategic position for the projection of American power. Hawaii had been under the control of American planters for over a decade but it was not until the Spanish-American War of 1898 that its strategic importance was fully appreciated. During the war the naval base at Pearl Harbor was instrumental in projecting US naval power to the western Pacific; following the war, moves were made for Hawaii's annexation.[3]

Ironically, the Navy's thinking was most succinctly captured by an Army man, General Arthur MacArthur, father of the more famous Douglas. Chief of the colonizing army that subjugated the country, MacArthur described the Philippines as,

> the finest group of islands in the world. Its strategic location is unexcelled by that of any other position in the globe. The China Sea, which separates it by something like 750 miles from the continent, is nothing more nor less than a safety moat. It lies on the flank of what might be called several thousand miles of coastline: it is in the center of that position. It is therefore relatively better placed than Japan, which is on a flank, and therefore remote from the other extremity; likewise India, on another flank. It affords a means of protecting American interests which with the very least output of physical power has the effect of a commanding position in itself to retard hostile action.[4]

So important, in fact, was a western Pacific presence for the institutional expansion of the Navy that even when the key Army officials favored withdrawal from the region in the 1930s, owing to the fact that the Philippines and other Pacific possessions of the US had become a 'strategic liability' in the face of Japan's growing might, the Navy blocked any consideration of leaving,[5] thus setting the stage for the American defeats in the early days of the Second World War.

The Clash of Empires

The United States' strategic dilemma in the 1930s stemmed from the inevitable collision between the irrepressible dynamics of the competing imperial projects of the US and the very country that Commodore Perry had forcibly brought into the modern world, Japan.

Initially, the two countries tried to arrive at a *modus vivendi* in 1905, with the Taft-Katsura Agreement, which gave Washington's recognition to 'Japan's "suzerainty over" Korea, in return for a Japanese disavowal of any aggressive intentions toward the Philippines'.[6] Non-interference being assured, at least for the time being, Korea and the Philippines were rapidly integrated into the competing empires. But the dynamics of empire-building could not be contained by diplomacy, and by the 1930s the struggle for control of China, the biggest prize of all in the imperial mind, triggered a chain of events that led to Pearl Harbor.

For most people in the Asia-Pacific, the Second World War was not a titanic struggle between democracy and fascism, as it was in Europe, but a conflict between imperial powers seeking domination over them. Pursuing their own goal of gaining sovereignty, some independence movements sided with Japan against their old colonial masters, as in Indonesia. Others, enticed by the old colonial power's promise of independence, fought the Japanese, as in the Philippines. And still others, as in Vietnam, fought both the old and the new imperialists.

The innocent civilian subjects of the competing empires became the main victims in a war that touched almost every nook and cranny of the region. The Second World War taught the people of the Asia-Pacific the painful truth in the old Malay saying that 'when the elephants clash, the grass gets trampled.' At least 250000 Chinese were bayoneted and butchered by the Japanese troops that entered Nanking. Manila was left the world's second most devastated city after Warsaw by aerial bombing and artillery fire from the American forces that liberated it from the Japanese; and 100000 of the city's 700000 people died from a combination of American artillery fire, crossfire from Japanese and American troops, and massacres perpetrated by fanatical ground troops of the Japanese Imperial Navy. About 160000 Okinawan men, women and children – almost a quarter of the island's population – were either killed by US fire or forced to commit suicide by their Japanese 'defenders'.

US air raids on Japan during the later stages of the war, which abandoned precision targeting in favor of indiscriminate bombing with incendiaries, were frankly described by no less than one of General Douglas MacArthur's key aides, Brigadier General Bonner Fellers, as 'one of the most ruthless and barbaric killings of non-combatants in all history'.[7] And, in what many contemporary historians now see as a tragedy with racial overtones, the US wiped out 140000 civilians with the atomic bombing of Hiroshima and Nagasaki in August 1945 – a fate that it chose not to visit on Nazi (but white) Germany.

Creating the Postwar Bases Network

American victory settled the first phase of the conflict between the two dominant countries in the region. While Japan faced its winter of defeat and discontent in the late 1940s, the US went about constructing a permanent military presence in the Pacific from the hundreds of bases that its troops had either wrested from Japan or built in the process of defeating Japan.

In Japan itself, the vanquished could hardly decline the victors' demand for base rights to Okinawa and other sites in the Ryukyu Islands, or resist the construction of hundreds of bases and facilities on the main islands.

In the Philippines, the returning Americans conditioned postwar reconstruction aid to the now independent republic on the extension of colonial economic and military privileges. Burdened with the terrible destruction wrought by the war, the new Philippine Republic amended its constitution to give Americans equal rights as Filipinos to exploit the economy and provided Washington a rent-free 99-year lease to 23 bases and installations.

In the central Pacific, outright annexation of the Marianas and other islands was proposed by the US Navy, which now considered the ocean its private preserve as a reward for the blood it had spilled to secure it. However, the Truman administration, sensitive to charges of colonialism at the very moment it was trying to nudge the British, French and Dutch to adopt less blatantly colonial forms of control, decided that Washington would settle for a US-administered 'United Nations Strategic Trusteeship'. But Truman also made it clear to his admirals that strategic trusteeship was *de facto* annexation:

Though the United States wants no territory or profit or selfish advantage out of this war, we are going to maintain the military bases necessary for the complete protection of our interests and of world peace. Bases which our military experts deem to be essential for our protection, we will acquire. We will acquire them by arrangements consistent with the United Nations charter.[8]

Forward Defense and Containment

The strategic rationale that lay behind the creation of a veritable pan-oceanic garrison state was 'forward defense', the essence of which was the maintenance of bases far from the continental United States to prevent wars from ever reaching the American heartland. Forward defense was merely an updated version of the Navy's prewar rationale that the defense of the US began 8000 miles west of San Francisco, in the Philippines. And just as his father had most succinctly expressed the Navy's rationale for acquiring the Philippines, it fell to Army General Douglas MacArthur to express most cogently the Navy's strategic vision for the postwar Pacific: 'The strategic boundaries of the United States were no longer along the western shore of North and South America; they lay along the eastern coast of the Asiatic continent.'[9]

Forward defense, however, was merely the military aspect of a broader impulse that united almost all sectors of the US establishment. With Europe in shambles and Britain on its knees, it was left to the United States, in their view, to provide a new international order. As articulated by Franklin Delano Roosevelt, that order had three key elements: a canopy of US military power coordinated with other big power 'trustees' would assure global security; the United Nations, largely an American creation, would preserve the peace; and the two Bretton Woods institutions, the International Monetary Fund and the World Bank, would underpin the free flow of capital and commodities that would prevent another depression and promote global prosperity.[10] Needless to say, prosperity, in this view, would benefit both the world and US business interests.

This vision of interventionist internationalism had its opponents, like the isolationist wing of the Republican Party. However, the isolationists opposed mainly American commitments to Europe, which they saw as continually distracting the United States from its 'manifest destiny'. That manifest destiny was in Asia, which they saw as America's natural field of expansion. While the 'Asialationists' opposed Roosevelt on many foreign policy issues, they nevertheless supported the dismantling of the French, British and Dutch empires in Asia that the Rooseveltian vision seemed to promise, since that would open up unprecedented opportunities for US business.

Most of the progressive aspects of Roosevelt's vision were undone by two developments, his death in 1945 and the eruption of the Cold War in 1947. Liberal internationalism gave way to the doctrine of 'containment' during the administration of Harry Truman. Developed in response to the expansionism that was perceived as inherent in Soviet communism, containment was initially formulated by George Kennan, head of the State Department's Policy Planning Staff, as a flexible strategy for meeting Soviet pressure at selected points that were seen as vital to US interests, such as Western Europe and Japan. But following the 'fall of China' to Mao Zedong's communists in 1949, Kennan's selective strategy was transformed by National Security Document (NSC) No. 68, released in 1950, into an ideological crusade to stop Soviet-inspired communism everywhere. Moreover NSC 68 envisioned that the struggle would go on until fundamental change was forced on the Soviet system.[11]

Containment represented the thorough militarization of US foreign policy. It reversed postwar demobilization, rearmed Germany, created the North Atlantic Treaty Organization's (NATO) military arm, quadrupled defense spending and institutionalized it at 5–10 per cent of GNP, and made the generalized insecurity associated with nuclear brinksmanship part of the psychology of everyday life in the US.

Among the victims of the triumph of containment ideology was the US commitment to anti-colonialism. Pressured by the overriding objective of creating a global alliance against the Soviet Union and China, the US began to backtrack from its support for trusteeship arrangements that it had vaguely endorsed as an alternative to colonies in Asia during the war.[12] Not only did the US *not* pressure Britain to decolonize but it actively supported its counterinsurgency campaign against a communist-led national liberation movement in Malaya in the late 1940s. In the case of the Netherlands, which was challenged by an independence movement in the East Indies, the 'United States consciously if discreetly supported the Dutch for the sake of European reconstruction, which benefited from access to Indonesia's raw materials.'[13] And in Indochina, Washington's fear of the Vietminh-led anti-colonial movement and its desire to persuade France to support German rearmament led it to swallow its hesitations and provide military aid for France's effort to reestablish its control over its colony.[14]

The outbreak of the Korean War in June 1950 provided the excuse to move the military containment line across the Sea of Japan to Korea, and later across the South China Sea to Indochina and Thailand. Diplomacy served as the handmaiden of warfare, as the US State Department devoted its energies to forging bilateral or collective military responses to the perceived communist threat. Bilateral and trilateral defense treaties were forged between the US and Japan, the Philippines, Australia-New Zealand, and Taiwan; and in 1954, Washington spearheaded the creation of the Southeast Asia Treaty

Organization (SEATO), which committed the US to the defense of Thailand and Vietnam.

While Europe was viewed by containment strategists as the chief area of contention between the 'Free World' and 'international communism', it was actually in Asia that wars erupted. In Korea in 1950–3 and again in Vietnam, from the early 1960s to 1975, Americans went to war believing they were out to stop Soviet-inspired communism from overrunning Asia. This crusading spirit was quintessentially captured by that most attractive of Cold Warriors, John F. Kennedy, in the speech he intended to deliver in Dallas in November 1963: '[W]e in this country … are – by destiny rather than by choice – the watchmen on the walls of world freedom.'[15] But in both countries, US troops found themselves up against nations-in-arms seeking unification and sovereignty. As Neil Sheehan put it with respect to Vietnam, 'Ho Chi Minh and his disciples became Communists through an accident of French politics. They were mandarins, Vietnamese aristocrats, the natural leaders of a people whom foreigners have repeatedly sought and failed to conquer and pacify.'[16]

The character of the Vietnamese resistance as more nationalist than communist eventually was admitted, even by some high US officials. But Washington persisted in the war, wrote John McNaughton, foreign policy adviser of Defense Secretary Robert McNamara, for the following reasons: '70 per cent – To avoid a humiliating US defeat (to our reputation as guarantor); 20 per cent – To keep South Vietnam (and the adjacent) territory from Chinese hands; 10 per cent – To permit the people of South Vietnam to enjoy a better, freer way of life.'[17]

The realization of the nationalist character of the Korean and Vietnamese resistance movements, did not, however, prevent the US from waging the American way of war, that is, unleashing the full technological might of the US against them. Close to 50000 Americans lost their lives in Korea and over 55000 in Vietnam. But, tragic though these numbers are, they cannot begin to compare with the devastation wreaked on Korea and Indochina by the US military machine.

Terror bombing and field combat killed about 1.5 million North Koreans in less than three years. The impact of 1400 tons of bombs and 23000 gallons of napalm was summed up, with terrifying cogency, by General O'Donnell, head of the Far Eastern Bombing Command, 'Everything is destroyed. There is nothing standing worthy of the name … There were no more targets in Korea.'[18]

From 1965 to 1971, US forces detonated 13 million tons of high explosive in Indochina, or the energy equivalent of 450 Hiroshima nuclear bombs. The total victory mindset which the Americans brought to the war with their use of sophisticated and deadly conventional weaponry prompted one perceptive observer to claim:

> If one seeks a model for the behavior of societies which have been subjected to nuclear bombardment, very probably our nearest actual approach to it can be found in the savage conflicts of Kampuchea, after this orgy of destruction. The line between the effect of modern high explosive munitions and that of nuclear weapons is in this moral sense not quite as absolute as has been supposed, and there is available much testimony on this matter from the Third World, if we have ears to hear it.[19]

It is testimony to the character of both Koreans and the peoples of Indochina that they dared such terrifying imperial retribution yet continued in their quest to become genuinely independent. This passion for nationhood on the part of the Vietnamese is perhaps best captured by Neil Sheehan in his bestselling book *A Bright Shining Lie*: 'There are a small number of such peoples on earth. The Irish are one. The Vietnamese another. The violence of their resistance forms history and legend to remind the living that they must never shame the dead.'[20]

Strategic Diplomacy as a Substitute for Force

US defeat in Vietnam led to the collapse of the military containment strategy on the Asian mainland. Washington pulled back its troops not only from Indochina but also from Thailand and focused once more on its offshore 'island-bastions' in the western Pacific, the Philippines, Japan and Guam. By 1976, the only US forces that remained on the mainland were an army division in South Korea, which enforced the continuing division of the peninsula. But contrary to the 'domino theory' that had guided US policy in Asia for two decades, American defeat did not lead to other mainland Asian countries falling to communism; on the contrary, with the cohesive element provided by the American threat gone, conflicting national interests led, in short order, to bitter conflict among Vietnam, China, Cambodia and the then Soviet Union, laying to rest the myth of a monolithic communist empire.

Nationalism, indeed, proved a more powerful force than communism, and in the 1970s, crisis for the communist bloc translated into opportunity for the US. Militarist containment was supplanted by Henry Kissinger and Richard Nixon's 'strategic diplomacy', which was designed to restore US influence through the sophisticated manipulation of the national interests of China, the Soviet Union and the US. This policy of diplomatic *realpolitik* was also adopted by the Carter administration, which completed the process of China's reintegration into the international community by extending to it diplomatic recognition at the same time that it tightened up on the diplomatic isolation and economic blockade of Vietnam, the two countries' common enemy. While Jimmy Carter's foreign policy foundered elsewhere, in East Asia his administration achieved success, from the point of view of shoring up US influence. By the end of the 1970s, strategic diplomacy had placed the US in the situation of being courted by the Southeast Asian nations, being encouraged by China to keep its military forces in the Pacific as a counter to the Soviet Union, and cooperating with China in a strategy of using the Khmer Rouge to 'bleed the Vietnamese white' in Cambodia.

Indeed, in a remarkable comeback, the US had regained the political initiative. As Richard Holbrooke, assistant secretary of state for East Asia, saw it:

> If we had predicted in 1975 that less than 5 years after the end of our long and traumatic involvement in the Indochina wars our position in the Pacific would be as strong as it is today, almost no one – optimist or pessimist – would have found the prediction credible ... The basic cause of tension in the region [has] become the rivalries among Communists. The non-Communist countries of Asia, relieved of many of the pressures caused by the old Cold War divisions, are experiencing unprecedented economic and political development.[21]

It was not an inconsiderable achievement, and the US had accomplished it without firing a shot – except, of course, indirectly, through its coldly calculated support of the Khmer Rouge-dominated 'Democratic Kampuchea' forces that were waging a proxy war for the US, China and the Association of Southeast Asian Nations (ASEAN) in the killing fields of Cambodia.

Naval Backlash

Success for the State Department, however, was retreat in the eyes of the Navy. The priority of diplomacy over military power resulted in a drawdown of US forces in the Pacific in the late 1970s, a move that stirred strong resentment in the Navy, which feared a reduction of its role as the principal guardian of US interests in the area. Profoundly threatened by the Carter administration's strategic reorientation of the Navy's function from power projection to 'sealane defense', the Navy found a valuable, if unlikely 'ally' in the Soviet Admiral Sergei Gorshkov. Gorshkov, cried the admirals, had built a 'blue-water navy', forged a strategy of 'forward defense', much like the US Navy's, and acquired a string of 'warm-water ports' to project Soviet naval power globally. Of all of Gorshkov's fleets, the Soviet flotilla in the Pacific was depicted as the largest and most threatening, while the Soviet naval base at Cam Ranh Bay in Vietnam – opposite Subic Naval Base in the Philippines – was said to be the most formidable of the Soviets' warm-water acquisitions.

In its offensive against the Carter administration, the Navy brass produced an updated version of Captain Mahan's rationale for a strong Navy: that the US, being an 'island state', could only be secure so long as it was supreme on the seas – that is, if it could send to the bottom any power or coalition of naval powers that dared challenge the US fleet. Especially in an era when there was 'strategic parity' in nuclear weapons and the Soviet Union was dominant on land, naval supremacy was the factor that would allow the United States to redress the overall balance of power.

With the advent of the Reagan administration in 1981, the doctrine of maritime supremacy was yoked to the resuscitated containment strategy as the Navy became the prime recipient of defense dollars in the massive military buildup. Much of this buildup was directed at the western Pacific, where the number of US surface warships rose by almost 100 per cent between 1980 and 1983. The most prominent feature of the naval buildup was a tremendous increase in nuclear firepower with the incorporation of nuclear-tipped cruise missiles and Trident intercontinental ballistic missiles into the Navy's armory.

The Navy also prepared warfighting scenarios with the Soviet fleet in the Indian Ocean, South China Sea and Northeast Asia, including a carrier-led aeronaval strike on Vladivostok. Central to these scenarios was the employment of nuclear weapons, given what strategist Paul Nitze called the 'growing and inevitable linkage' between conventional and nuclear weapons in naval warfare.[22]

Two elements in the strategy of maritime supremacy, in particular, were especially destabilizing: the acceptance of the possibility of 'limited nuclear war' and a willingness to entertain the 'first strike option'. Indeed, the possibility of a limited naval war with the Soviet Union in the Pacific was not only regarded as a possibility but accepted as a probability by some Pentagon officials. As Marine General Bernard Trainor told the Naval War College on 21 June 1984:

Given what's happening with the Soviets in their force projection, we probably in some point in our lifetime will clash with them. Now there's enormous dangers involved with that. The dangers of escalation. Both sides know it. It'll probably be an unintended clash and when it happens, there will be a rush on the part of both sides and the rest of the world who are so nervous about two elephants bumping and getting stamped. The odds are that any such clash would be short-lived. If it is short-lived, somebody's going to come away with the perception that one side bested the other. The world better get the perception that we bested them, because the fight will be on 'our turf.' In our role as world leader, if in the outbacks of the world the Soviets are perceived to have bested the United States, then we have invited a great deal of international trouble for ourselves.[23]

In such a war, Navy Secretary John Lehman told the same gathering, 'Who gets to shoot first will have more to do with who wins than any [other] factor.'[24]

In planning for a limited war, the Navy, under the pugnacious Lehman, became increasingly obsessed with the 'Vladivostok strike scenario' – an assault on the Far Eastern homeport of the Soviet Pacific Fleet. In a remarkably candid disclosure of Seventh Fleet war plans, the joint chiefs of staff 1983 Posture Statement noted that in the event of war, a major US advantage would be the ability of US forces in Northeast Asia to bottle up the Soviet Pacific Fleet at Vladivostok. To get from Vladivostok to the open Pacific, the Soviet fleet needed to pass through one of three straits cutting through the Japanese archipelago, the widest of which was only 160 kilometers across. US advantage would be translated into concentrated attacks on Vladivostok and on Soviet ships traversing the Japanese straits by the Seventh Fleet, 'which would try to outmaneuver the opponent and to overwhelm him in one location rather than fighting all across the vast expanses of the Pacific Ocean'.[25]

Not surprisingly, the naval buildup and the 'new' Navy thinking provoked the Soviets to warn the Americans that, from their point of view, nuclear war could not be a limited affair, and under the conditions of local inferiority in which they found themselves in the north Pacific, they would have no choice but to escalate to all-out nuclear war. And, also not surprisingly, the Navy's nuclear rhetoric provided the impetus for the rapid spread of the movement for denuclearization and demilitarization in a region that had just emerged from the Vietnam War.

4

US Pacific Command Today

In 1992, 17 years after the end of the Vietnam War, the US military once again had, thanks to the military buildup of the Reagan years, a commanding presence in the Asia-Pacific.

Imperial Reach

The dimensions of the US Pacific Command are impressive: 300000 servicemen and women, about half of them deployed in the western Pacific; roughly half of the 580 warships of the US Navy; two-thirds of the US Marine Corps; two Army divisions, one of them forward-deployed in Korea; several tactical fighter wings of the US Air Force; and until recently, one wing of the US Strategic Air Command operating out of Guam.[1]

Spread out over 300 bases and facilities from San Diego to Diego Garcia, and financed by at least $60 billion, Pacific Command is an integrated and extremely secretive complex that occupies lands and waters belonging to five independent states and the vast expanse of Micronesia. Needless to say, the host-states – South Korea, Japan, the Philippines and Australia – exercise merely nominal sovereignty over the pieces of their national territory that are incorporated into this complex.

The northern anchor of this pan-oceanic garrison state is Japan–Korea; the southern anchor is the Philippine base complex; and Guam and the other US territories in Micronesia serve as the great rear area. Traditionally used for projecting power into Northeast Asia, the Chinese heartland and Southeast Asia during the Cold War, the Pacific basing system is increasingly utilized to project US forces to the Indian Ocean and Persian Gulf as the US builds up a permanent naval and ground presence in the Middle East.

Japan plays host to about 105 US installations, including 20 major bases, and close to 50000 troops. But it is not only its hosting US bases and allocating $45000 to support each US serviceperson serving there that has made Japan the United States' most important ally in the Pacific. Other important US assets are the Japanese military, which has the third largest military budget in the world; Japan's pro-US political leadership, which so far has subordinated its foreign policy

20

to that of the US; and Japanese industry, which now provides the Pentagon with critical high-tech components, such as advanced microchips, for use in US weapons systems.

The only US military presence on the Asian mainland is in Korea. Though all nuclear weapons are reported to have been recently removed from South Korea,[2] there are no plans to remove the US military contingent, which now numbers about 44000 troops. Located in the narrow 50-mile zone between Seoul and the Demilitarized Zone, 13000 of these troops constitute a 'tripwire' in the event of a conflict with North Korea. In the view of an increasing number of Koreans, the role of the US troops is to maintain the 44-year-old division of the Korean nation and make it difficult to achieve reunification except under terms favorable to South Korea and the US.

Before it received its notice of termination from the Philippine Senate, Subic Naval Base – a huge military complex with nine separate commands, ranging from a massive armory to a state-of-the-art ship-repair facility – was the United States' most valuable base in the Pacific, being centrally located to project power to Northeast Asia, the Chinese and Indochinese mainland, and the Indian Ocean and Persian Gulf. While the Philippine base complex served principally as the logistical axis for the Vietnam War effort in the 1960s, by the mid-1970s, its main role became that of projecting American power to the Indian Ocean and Persian Gulf. During the US naval buildup in 1987–8, at the height of the Iran–Iraq War, 75 per cent of the ships deployed to the Gulf were Seventh Fleet vessels operating out of Subic. And during the recent Gulf War, Subic served as a critical refueling and reprovisioning center for thousands of warbound US troops.

Micronesia serves as a totally US-controlled rear zone of 7.8 million square kilometers of ocean, the strategic center of which is the heavily fortified island of Guam. The region's role as a fallback area is now likely to become a reality with the withdrawal of US forces from the Philippines. Micronesia has also served as a test site for US weaponry. Between 1946 and 1958, the US triggered at least 66 nuclear explosions on the Marshall Islands. Since the late 1950s, Kwajalein Atoll in the Marshalls has served as the impact area or 'catcher's mitt' for virtually all long-range rockets tested, including the Minuteman, Poseidon, Polaris, Trident and the MX, which are fired from Vandenburg Air Force Base and Point Mugu Naval Station in California.

While fixed bases are important, it is the vast mobile basing complex comprising the Seventh Fleet that serves as the cutting edge of American power in the Pacific and Indian oceans. And in conveying its imperial reach, numbers cannot match Admiral George Steele's Kiplingesque description of a typical day in the life of this massive flotilla:

Figure 4.1: US Military Forces, Weapons and Installations in the Pacific, 1992

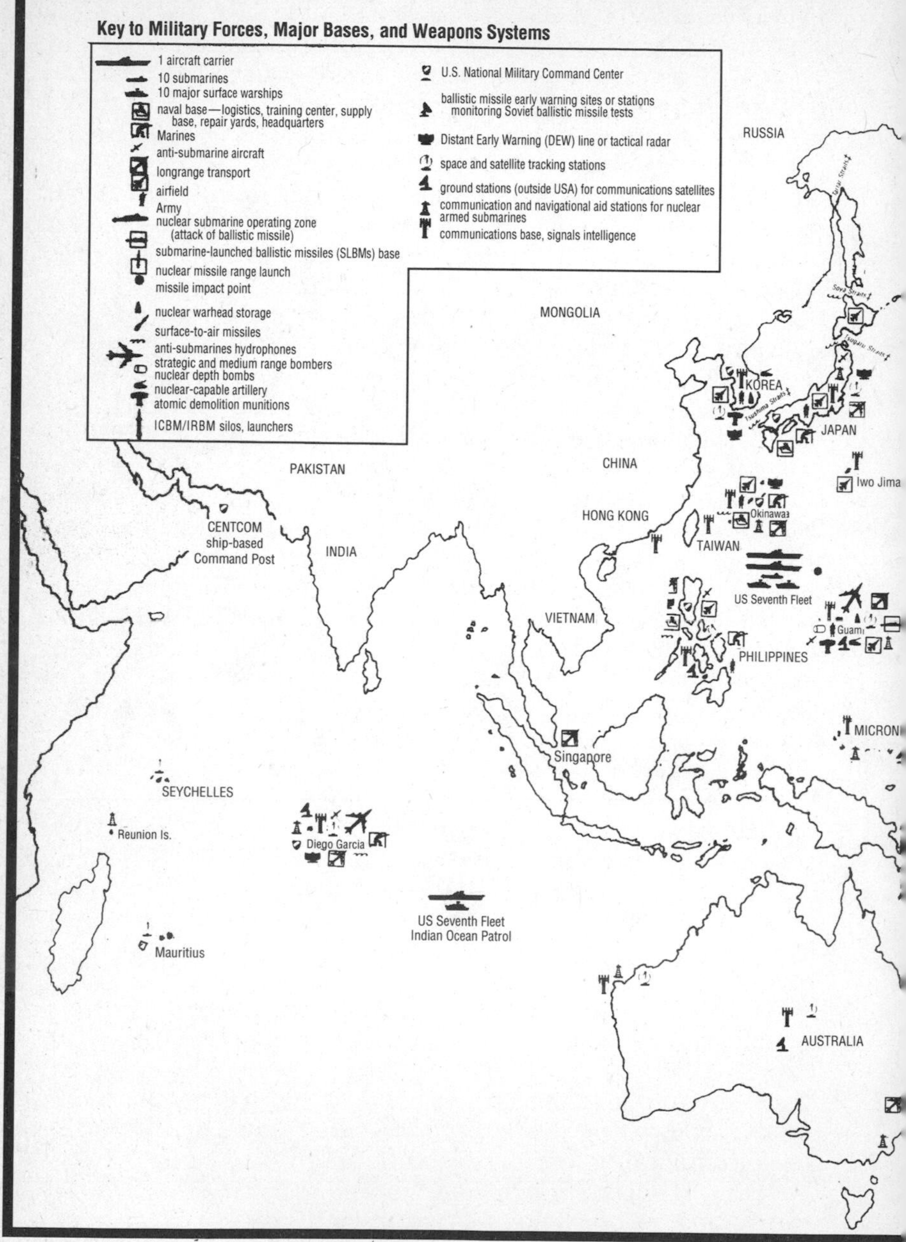

Key to Military Forces, Major Bases, and Weapons Systems

Source: Nautilus Pacific Action Research, 1992

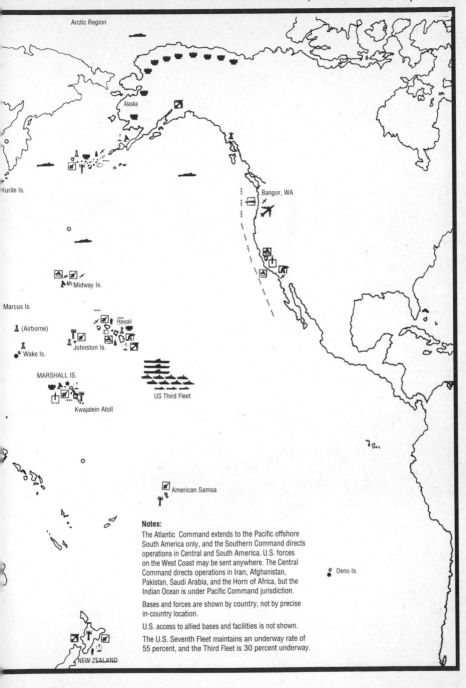

Arctic Region

Alaska

Bangor, WA

Kurile Is.

Midway Is.

Marcus Is.

(Airborne)

Wake Is.

Hawaii

Johnston Is.

MARSHALL IS.

Kwajalein Atoll

US Third Fleet

American Samoa

Oeno Is.

NEW ZEALAND

Notes:

The Atlantic Command extends to the Pacific offshore South America only, and the Southern Command directs operations in Central and South America. U.S. forces on the West Coast may be sent anywhere. The Central Command directs operations in Iran, Afghanistan, Pakistan, Saudi Arabia, and the Horn of Africa, but the Indian Ocean is under Pacific Command jurisdiction.

Bases and forces are shown by country, not by precise in-country location.

U.S. access to allied bases and facilities is not shown.

The U.S. Seventh Fleet maintains an underway rate of 55 percent, and the Third Fleet is 30 percent underway.

On a given day in the Seventh Fleet, one can find several ships well east of Japan entering or leaving the Seventh Fleet area of responsibility. An anti-submarine warfare exercise is in progress on Tokyo Bay. An aircraft carrier with her destroyer-screen and a submarine are exercising in the Okinawa operating area, while another carrier task force group is in Subic for maintenance. A third carrier task force is visiting Mombasa, Kenya. An amphibious exercise involving ships and submarines of Ready Group Bravo is in progress on the coast of Korea ... and ship visits are in progress in Hong Kong; Beppu, Japan; Kaohsiung, Taiwan; Manila; Sattahip, Thailand; Singapore; Penang, Malaysia ... Patrol planes of Task Force 72 are conducting ocean surveillance in the Indian Ocean in support of the carrier task force group there and range along the Asian mainland at a respectful distance on the lookout for unusual happenings ...[3]

Table 4.1: US Military Presence in the Pacific Theater, by Location, as of 31 March 1990

Location	Military	Civilian	Total	Dependents	Total	Percent
Land Based:						
Japan	47783	4987	52770	50370	103140	20.0
Korea	44072	2404	46476	16002	62478	12.1
Philippines	13522	1311	14833	18419	33252	6.4
Other Foreign	2102	123	2225	1428	3653	0.7
Subtotal[a]	107479	8825	116304	86219	202523	39.2
Hawaii	44531	19153	63684	54080	117764	22.8
Alaska	22548	3930	26478	31323	57801	11.2
Guam	7165	4122	11287	10348	21635	4.2
Other[b]	430	380	810	21	831	0.2
Subtotal	74674	27585	102259	95772	198031	38.4
Total land based	182153	36410	218563	181991	400554	77.6
Afloat forces	115814	[c]	115814	[d]	115814	22.4
Grand Total	297987	36410	334397	181991	516388[a]	100.0

Notes: Percent of military personnel assigned to combat positions: 71.5.

[a] For foreign locations, dependents figure includes dependents of military and civilian personnel; for US locations, the figure includes military dependents only.

[b] Includes other US locations and the Republic of the Marshall Islands, as well as some Department of Defense personnel whose specific locations were unidentified.

[c] Not applicable.

[d] Dependents of naval personnel assigned to ships, submarines and aircraft are included in land based dependent figures. We did not count dependents of afloat personnel based in California or Washington state.

Source: US General Accounting Office, *Military Presence: US Personnel in the Pacific Theatre*, Report No. GAO/NSIAD-91-192 (Washington, DC: GAO, August 1991)

Sexual Labor and the Military Economy

From Mombasa in Kenya to Yokosuka in Japan, the Seventh Fleet has spawned in its ports of call thriving centers for the purchase and sale of sexual labor, which operate with the blessing of US naval authorities, who regard sexual recreation as necessary for the morale of the troops. All in all, an estimated 30000 women are said to be regularly involved in the sale of sexual labor to American sailors, soldiers, marines and airmen throughout the Asia-Pacific. But with rising living standards in South Korea and Japan making prostitution less attractive as a way of earning money, it is women from the Philippines and Thailand who increasingly fill the bars and brothels near the bases in many parts of the Asia-Pacific. In Okinawa, for instance, observes Carolyn Bowen Francis,

> between 400 and 500 Filipinas are working in seedy, aging clubs lining the streets outside the major military bases ... Six local production agencies work with their counterparts in the Philippines to insure the continuing supply of young Filipinas to clubs around the bases. The women come on entertainer visas that allow them to work in Okinawa a total of six months before returning home. Authorities declare the whole operation is completely 'legal'...[4]

The satellite cities of Olongapo and Angeles that adjoin Subic Naval Base and Clark Air Force Base, respectively, in the Philippines, were probably the biggest prostitution hubs catering to the US military in Asia. More than 500 clubs, bars, sauna baths and other entertainment facilities now face closure as the US Navy pulls out of Subic Bay, while many of the 450 establishments in Angeles that used to provide sexual entertainment for airmen from Clark Air Force Base have already shut down. At its height, Olongapo, claimed Owen Wilkes and Marie Leadbetter, had 'what the US military regard as the best bar and brothel facilities of any US base in the world – and keeping up force morale is not a trivial military objective'.[5]

With the advent of AIDS, such centers of sexual labor have become entry points for the virus in a number of countries. For example, 40 per cent of women who work in brothels in the province around Pattaya in Thailand, which services US sailors, are HIV positive.

Beyond prostitution, the bases have spawned a subeconomy whose other main components are entertainment, drugs, extortion and arms smuggling. While the Pentagon used to claim that it pumped $500 million a year into the Philippines, much of this swirled around and supported these underground economic activities, which are hardly the pillars on which to build a healthy economy. Moreover, being used for consumption of services rather than for investment in productive activities, the military dollar often sparked inflation rather than genuine economic growth in the areas surrounding the bases.

A negative economic impact of a different sort accompanied the conversion of Micronesia into a strategic military colony in the late 1940s. Closed off to the outside world to serve as a laboratory for the postwar nuclear testing program, economies which had thrived under Japanese control in the prewar period languished under the stultifying control of the Navy and, later, the inept rule of the Department of the Interior. 'The physical infrastructure of roads, hospitals, docking facilities, power systems, and sanitation', claims Micronesia specialist Mary Lord, 'is not yet back to the level of pre-World War II.'[6] Thus it is hardly a cause for surprise that nineteenth-century diseases like cholera, tuberculosis and leprosy made a comeback and broke out in epidemic proportions in the Federated States of Micronesia.

Instead of promoting 'the economic advancement and self sufficiency of the inhabitants ... [through] the development of fisheries, agriculture, and industries', as stipulated by Article 6 of the Trusteeship Agreement, the US created welfare states that live almost entirely on government appropriations from Washington. The US government has become the islands' main employer, with tragic political and cultural consequences. 'The US policy of non-development has created a huge class of government employees whose ability to eat depends on the continuance of dependence on the United States', asserts anthropologist Catherine Lutz.[7]

It is thus not surprising that the central Pacific territories have opted for a continuing colonial link with the United States in the form of a 'Compact of Free Association'. It is also not surprising that, cut off from their traditions and bereft of a productive relationship to their lands and waters, teenagers throughout Micronesia have taken to suicide, in rates that far exceed that of the United States.[8]

In Search of Enemies

It is ironic that at the very zenith of its power, the US military presence has lost its *raison d'être*, with the end of the Cold War and the Russian Pacific Fleet's withdrawal from unilateral military competition with the United States Seventh Fleet. Unlike in Europe, however, where plans for the withdrawal of US forces and the closure of bases are underway with the conclusion of the Cold War, the Pentagon has been much less enthusiastic about withdrawing from East Asia.

True, in the face of increasing congressional pressure to match base closings in Europe and the US with similar cuts in the Pacific, Defense Secretary Richard Cheney announced in 1990 a 10 per cent reduction in US forces in the western Pacific. But this would merely lower the number of troops in South Korea and Japan from 100000 to 90000. And it would affect mainly Air Force and Army units, not the Navy, which is the principal service in the area. The Navy will continue to deploy 150000 personnel on ships and several thousand more as shore crew in its Pacific bases.

Moreover, the withdrawal of nuclear weapons from South Korea and removal of nuclear-tipped cruise missiles from Navy ships recently announced by the US are not a response to the regional pressure for demilitarization but part of a negotiating strategy for nuclear arms reduction impelled by a fear of the consequences of the unravelling of centralized command of nuclear weapons in the former Soviet Union.

The major changes in the US posture in the region are, in fact, involuntary: the closing down of Clark Air Base in the Philippines by a volcanic explosion and the termination of US naval access to Subic Bay by the Philippine Senate.

The rhetoric of reduction is loud, but, for the most part, as Paul Kreisberg notes, 'the signs are that the same old threats and the same old arguments for force levels and facilities are being laid out on the interagency bargaining table.'[9] Indeed, more military energy has been devoted to the task of looking for new, credible foes than to formulating plans for a substantive reduction of forces. The Pentagon, and the Navy in particular, remain the key obstacles to a genuine winding down of the Cold War in Asia.

In line with the strategic perspective laid down by *Discriminate Deterrence*, the 1988 'post-containment' document produced by the Presidential Commission on Long-Term Integrated Strategy, Pacific Command has tried to reorient the US posture from deterring the vanishing Soviet threat to containing alleged 'terrorist threats' emanating from the Third World.

Kim Il-Sung of North Korea is the 'most-favored-enemy' in the eyes of the US military, for them a Pacific version of Saddam Hussein. As Admiral Charles Larson, commander in chief of Pacific Command, recently claimed in testimony at the US Congress, 'North Korea poses the greatest immediate danger to regional stability.'[10] Or in the more graphic words of General Colin Powell, head of the joint chiefs of staff, 'I'm running out of demons ... I'm down to Fidel Castro and Kim Il-Sung.' The recent controversy over North Korea's nuclear reactor at Yeongbyon may stem less from genuine concern over North Korea's ability to manufacture a nuclear bomb than from the search for a credible regional threat.

Figure 4.2: Military Confrontation on the Korean Peninsula

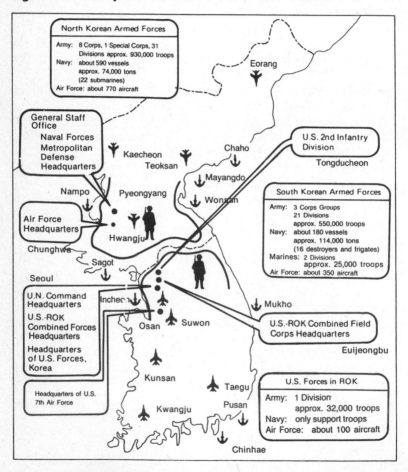

Source: Japan Defense Agency, *Defense of Japan 1990* (Tokyo: Japan Times Ltd, 1990), p. 61

But the search for a substitute enemy does not end with Kim. Indeed, it would be hard to sell the view that the main purpose of the massive American presence is to deter the non-nuclear army of an isolated country whose main allies, China and the Soviet Union, have thrown in their lot with South Korea and the US.

There are other active candidates. In arguing for the maintenance of US bases in the Philippines, for instance, some defense analysts claim that these outposts would be necessary to check the future ambitions of China and Indonesia. 'Indian expansionism' has also been mentioned as a threat not only to South Asia but also to Southeast Asia. Indeed, General Dynamics – one of the Pentagon's top contractors – has singled out India as one of the key targets for the next generation of cruise missiles. In a 52-page briefing paper, the company, claims one report, 'outlined a scenario for the year 2000 in which India and Pakistan are spoiling for a war over Kashmir. The US would intervene to prevent an Indian nuclear strike against Pakistan and use 307 cruise missiles to neutralize targets in India.'[11]

While the intensified demonization of Korea is predictable and the speculation about India and US ally Indonesia as strategic enemies borders on the amusing, many have been surprised that key figures in Pacific Command are really deeply worried, not by a Third World challenger, but by their chief ally in the region, Japan. In an interview that official Washington criticized as 'indiscreet', Major General Henry Stackpole, commander of Marine forces in Japan, told the *Washington Post* that the objective of the US military presence in that country is to prevent Tokyo from beefing up 'what is already a very, very potent military'. Already, he claimed, the Japanese have 'achieved the Greater Asia Co-Prosperity Sphere economically, without guns'. Thus, 'No one wants a rearmed, resurgent Japan. So we are the cap in the bottle, if you will.'[12]

Stackpole's comments did not so much reflect an opportunistic search for a suitable enemy as manifest a profound psychological unease over the increasing discrepancy over the stated mission of Pacific Command and the results of its successfully performing that mission. While the US military presence served to promote the expansion of US trade with Asia and the growth of US investment there in the first postwar decades, in the last few years it has served mainly as a canopy for the rapid integration of the Asia-Pacific region around the needs of Japan.

This contradictory situation in which one power is militarily supreme while the other is economically dominant is a recipe for insta-bility. But, as we shall discuss more fully in Part III, it may also translate into opportunity for the creation of a new order built on demilitarization and respect for the sovereignty of Asia-Pacific nations.

5

Missionary Democracy and US Foreign Policy: the Uneasy Partnership

America's presence in the Pacific cannot be reduced solely to the imperatives of strategic extension and economic expansion. There has always been a strong element of missionary idealism in US expansionism. Missionaries bearing the Christian message were but a step behind merchants and sailors in Hawaii, China, the Philippines and Japan.

But the positive impulses of the missionary spirit were all too often harnessed to further the goals of strategic and economic lobbies. Indeed, a moral gloss to a colonial or interventionist project was necessary to give it popular legitimacy among the American people. Perhaps the crudest – and certainly the most transparent – attempt in this regard was President William McKinley's justifying the annexation of the Philippines on the grounds that the (already Roman Catholic) Filipinos had to be 'Christianized'. Yet there was always a great tension, if not contradiction, between expansionism and idealism. In resolving this tension – that is, producing a moral rationale that would make Americans feel good about colonialism and intervention – the US experience in the Philippines was central. Especially during the postwar containment era, the Philippine experience would serve as a model for US policy toward the Third World.

The Philippine Paradigm

When the US annexed the Spanish colony of the Philippines after defeating Asia's first modern movement for national liberation at the turn of the century, it was faced with a unique problem.[1] Colonialism was already regarded as a politically antiquated and morally questionable system among significant sectors of the populations of western countries. But even more important, as the powerful Anti-Imperialist League pointed out, the US itself had been born, just 125 years earlier, in an anti-colonial struggle and as a democratic republic.

The solution to this dilemma was classically American: 'Preparing the Filipinos for responsible independence' by exporting the institutions of American democracy became the formula for legitimizing nearly 48 years of colonial rule.

A wholesale transplant of formal political institutions began shortly after the conquest, with US colonial authorities and missionaries serving as instructors and the Philippine elite playing the role of student. By the time of independence in 1946, the Philippine political system was a mirror image of the American, with its presidential leadership, separation of powers and two-party system.

Yet, in terms of real power, the Philippine democratic system was really a marriage between the feudal paternalism of the Philippine elite and Chicago-style machine politics. Electoral politics was enthusiastically embraced by the regional landed elites that the US had detached from the national liberation struggle and formed into a national ruling class. But it was hardly a belief in representative government that made the elite eager students. The main incentive was that democratic elections provided a means for a fractious class to compete, relatively peacefully, for political office and alternate in power. For the poor majority of Filipinos, elections afforded the illusion of democratic choice – that is, the ability to choose among different elite candidates and elite political parties. Democracy did not extend to the economic sphere, and the play of electoral politics unfolded above an immobile class structure, whose distribution of income was one of the worst in Asia.

Nonetheless, having created the local elite, having tied that elite to the US economically by providing access to the US market for its agricultural products, and having socialized both the elite and the population at large to formal democratic practices, the US felt confident that independence would not result in an unfriendly country.

Containment and the Democratic Mission

With the onset of the Cold War, the Philippines provided a paradigm for America's approach to other countries in the region. For the contradiction that the US experienced 50 years earlier upon its annexation of the Philippines – the conflict between America's disdain for colonies and its desire for control – was now reproduced on a global scale. 'The US', Sheehan points out, 'did not seek colonies as such.'

> Having overt colonies was not acceptable to the American political conscience. Americans were convinced that their imperial system did not victimize foreign peoples ... It was thought to be neither

exploitative, like the nineteenth-century-style colonialism of the European empires, nor destructive of personal freedom and other worthy human values, like the totalitarianism of the Soviet Union and China and their Communist allies. Instead of formal colonies, the United States sought local governments amenable to American wishes and, where possible, subject to indirect control from behind the scenes. Washington wanted native regimes that would act as surrogates for American power. The goal was to achieve the sway over allies and dependencies which every imperial nation needs to work its will in world affairs without the structure of old-fashioned colonialism.[2]

And as in the case of the Philippines, formal democracy controlled by US-allied elites provided both the mechanism of influence and the justification for intervention in the affairs of a Third World country. As Frances Fitzgerald pointed out in her classic book *Fire in the Lake*,

The idea that the mission of the United States was to build democracy around the world had become a convention of American politics in the 1950s. Among certain circles it was more or less assumed that democracy, that is, electoral democracy combined with private ownership and civil liberties, was what the United States had to offer the Third World. Democracy provided not only the basis for American opposition to Communism but the practical method to make sure that opposition worked.[3]

In Korea and Vietnam, many US officials tried to set up systems of representative democracy that they thought would serve as the best antidote to communism. That they were working through reactionary elites that did not believe in democracy in the first place was overlooked. The CIA officer Edward Lansdale, for instance, saw in the feudal patriarch Ngo Dinh Diem a reformist democrat in the mold of Ramon Magsaysay, with whose collaboration he had crushed the communist insurgency in the Philippines in the early 1950s. But neither Vietnam nor Korea was the Philippines, where the elite had been socialized into electoral competition by the American colonial authorities over a 50-year period. The Korean and Vietnamese ruling groups had collaborated with despotic colonial powers – Japan in the case of Korea, France in the case of Vietnam. In two intensely nationalistic countries, the Americans were perceived as stepping into the shoes of the old colonialists, and their 'democratic' clients – Rhee Syng-Man in Korea, Ngo Dinh Diem in Vietnam – were mocked as reactionaries masquerading as democrats.

The failure to implant formal elite democratic regimes that would stabilize Asian societies caught up in nationalist revolution left many US officials disenchanted with the ideology of missionary democracy. Thus anti-communism soon overshadowed democratic credentials as the key criterion for choosing allies. The role of Japan as the industrial bastion of anti-communist containment in Northeast Asia persuaded Douglas MacArthur's occupation government in Japan to stop dismantling the financial-industrial monopolies associated with the war effort and allow figures linked with Japanese militarism back into positions of influence. In Vietnam, the US itself encouraged a military coup against the man they had once led themselves to believe was a democrat, Ngo Dinh Diem. In Korea, the US welcomed the military regime of General Park Chung-Hee, which took power in 1962, as a stabilizing development. And in Indonesia, the CIA chose to interpret President Sukarno's radical nationalism as pro-communism and proceeded to wage an eight-year campaign to dislodge him, a process which culminated in 1965 in a CIA-supported coup that sparked the massacre of at least 500000 suspected communists and their families.[4]

The Authoritarian Alternative

The new Korean regime and the military governing elite that took power in Brazil in 1964 provided the prototype of the new mechanisms of neocolonial control that the US officials were looking for in the face of increasing evidence of the failure of missionary democracy: a military-technocrat leadership that depoliticized the lower classes through repression but at the same time sought to build legitimacy by imposing a program of economic development. 'Authoritarian leadership for development' became the theme of a work that eventually became the handbook for a new generation of officials at the State Department, the Agency for International Development, and the US-dominated World Bank: Samuel Huntington's *Political Order in Changing Societies*. In the 'chaotic' Third World, the Harvard professor argued, it was quixotic to expect democratic government where there were no democratic traditions. There, the building of strong central authority must necessarily precede the question of democratic representation.[5]

Then, in the early 1970s, US officials' faith in democratic government received an even greater setback when democratic efforts to achieve genuine social change appeared to move beyond the parameters of elite democracy in two countries that American officials had long glorified as 'showcases of democracy': Chile and the Philippines.

In 1970, the system of formal democracy allowed the ascent to power of the government of Salvador Allende, which declared its intention to nationalize the huge US copper corporations and lead the country to socialism. As mass movements for democratic change accelerated in the Philippines in 1970–2, the Nixon-Kissinger administration's attitude toward Philippine democracy was undoubtedly affected by what they perceived as democracy's failure to prevent the left from coming to power in Chile. This frame of mind was captured by Henry Kissinger's classic comment on US policy toward the Allende government: 'I don't see why we should let a country go Marxist because its people are irresponsible.'[6]

Thus, when Ferdinand Marcos declared martial law in 1972 and abolished the 26-year old system of formal democracy in the Philippines, Washington was not about to complain about the demise of the form of government it had implanted seven decades back. As the staff of the US Senate Foreign Relations Committee discovered:

> We found few if any Americans who took the position that the demise of individual rights and democratic institutions would adversely affect US institutions. In the first place, these democratic institutions were considered severely deficient. In the second place, whatever US interests were – or are – they apparently are not thought to be related to the preservation of democratic processes ... US officials appear prepared to accept that the strengthening of presidential authority ... will enable President Marcos to introduce needed stability; that these objectives are in our interest; and that ... military bases and a familiar government in the Philippines are more important than the preservation of democratic institutions, which were imperfect at best.[7]

This was classic *realpolitik*, a political accommodation to what Kissinger saw as a truth: that American interests were sometimes best served by repressive Third World allies. American foreign policy, however, could never be based entirely on the blatant *realpolitik* that Kissinger represented. With the US being identified with a growing number of authoritarian governments in East Asia and Latin America, the idealist dimension of US foreign policy was asserted by liberals, sections of the Democratic Party, church groups and ordinary Americans. Dovetailing into the powerful anti-war movement of the early 1970s, the 'human rights' movement provided the impetus for the foreign policy platform of Jimmy Carter, who promised to cut off all aid to repressive governments.

But upon becoming president, Carter was quickly and successfully pressured by the national security establishment to subordinate his human rights policy to 'strategic concerns'. The Army managed to gather broad bureaucratic support to halt Carter's plan to withdraw the remaining US division in Korea. And soon 'stability' and 'strategic interests' were being invoked by Carter himself to make the shah of Iran, Marcos of the Philippines and Park Chung-Hee of Korea exceptions to the human rights policy. When Korean troops normally under US command massacred over 2000 civilians at Kwangju after being released from their regular deployment by the US Army commander, the Carter administration did not reprimand its military proconsul.

With the accession to power of the Reagan administration in 1981, Kissinger's 'national security' justification for supporting US dictatorial clients and the embarrassing contradiction between the Carter administration's human rights rhetoric and its actual policy gave way to a full-blown ideological justification for supporting authoritarianism: the 'Kirkpatrick Doctrine'.

Attempting to make support for repressive regimes morally justifiable and ideologically acceptable, Jeane Kirkpatrick, who served as Ronald Reagan's United Nations ambassador, argued:

> The fabric of authority unravels quickly when the power and status of the man at the top are undermined or eliminated. The longer the autocrat has held power, and the more pervasive his personal influence, the more dependent a nation's institutions will be on him. Without him, the organized life of the society will collapse, like an arch from which the keystone has been removed.[8]

This was a transparent appeal to the conservative philosophy of Edmund Burke. But Vice-President George Bush preferred Orwellian language to Burkean imagery when he toasted Marcos during a visit to Manila in this fashion: 'We love you, sir ... We love your adherence to democratic rights and processes.'

The movement away from dictatorship to democracy in the 1980s in Asia and Latin America took place in spite of rather than because of the Reagan administration. For the most part, as in the case of both the Philippines in 1986 and South Korea in 1987, the US stuck to discredited dictatorships until the very last moment, when it became clear that its client regimes would be toppled. At that point, in an attempt to salvage prestige and influence, it pressured both Ferdinand Marcos and Chun Doo-Hwan to resign.

While reverting to the rhetoric of missionary democracy, US policy today has an uneasy coexistence with Third World democracies. So long as democratic rule contains change within acceptable limits – like the replacement of one faction of elite politicians by another, as in the Philippines – the US can accommodate to democratic government, if not support it. But when democracy in Asia, Africa and Latin America again becomes a means by which the majority seeks to replace traditional economic and social structures, then Washington's likely response is to side once again with local efforts at authoritarian stabilization.

If there is a model for Asian governance that guides Washington today, that would most likely be Singapore, where stability is imposed by authoritarian rule and dissent is defused by a degree of prosperity.

6

The Economic Dimension of Expansionism: from Agro-mineral Exploitation to Export-oriented Industrialization

While the mainspring of US expansion in the Asia-Pacific was principally strategic in character, economic expansion swiftly followed. The US Navy's Far Eastern Squadron enforced the American 'right' to the exploitation of China side by side with the other colonial powers under the 'Open Door Policy'. At the same time, American annexation of Hawaii and the Philippines allowed the integration of islands rich in agricultural and natural resources into the US economy.

Colonial Exploitation

For American entrepreneurs, Hawaii provided a model for the economic exploitation of the Philippines. There, descendants of Protestant missionaries had turned their attention to the more mundane activity of cultivating sugar and pineapple and exporting them to the United States. By the 1880s, this *haole* (white) planter class controlled the economic life of the nation, and it then moved to replace the Hawaiian monarchy that had treated it hospitably. This process was completed in 1898 with the annexation of Hawaii and the appointment of Sanford Dole of the famous planter family as governor.[1]

As in Hawaii, US economic expansion in the Philippines prior to the Second World War followed the typical colonial pattern of monopolizing trade with the colony, focusing investment on producing agricultural commodities and extracting raw materials for export to the United States, and reserving the small domestic market for US-manufactured imports.[2]

In just 11 years after Washington imposed free trade between the US and the Philippines, the US share of Philippine trade leaped from one-quarter in 1909 to two-thirds in 1921; and, nearing the end of the colonial period in the late 1930s, four-fifths of Philippine exports ended up in the United States, while two-thirds of Philippine imports were supplied by the latter. This *structural dependency* persisted long after independence was granted in 1946.

From $72 million in 1911, American investment rose to $175 million in the mid-1930s towards the end of the colonial period. The bulk of American investment flowed not to activities that would tap the local market but to producing agricultural and raw material exports. Del Monte Corporation extended its pineapple operations from Hawaii to the Philippines, and by the 1930s it had become the biggest agribusiness operation in the country, controlling over 10000 hectares of land. A close relationship forged between the colonial government's Forestry Department and American logging interests made the colony Southeast Asia's prime exporter of timber, with the US being the principal market. American firms also came to dominate sugar milling, gold mining, hemp cordage-making, and coconut refining and processing.

By the end of the colonial period, the Philippines was supplying slightly over 5 per cent of America's total imports, but accounted for only 2.3 per cent of US exports. This skewed development pattern – in which the colony's importance lay less in its being a market for the colonial power's manufactures than in its being a source of agricultural commodities and raw materials, as a consequence of generalized poverty and underdevelopment – was reflected in US trade with East Asia as a whole: in the early 1930s, the Far East accounted for 24 per cent of America's imports but only 15 per cent of its exports.

The socio-economic realities underlying trade figures were also reflected by investment figures. American investment concentrated in wealthy markets like Britain and Europe, since in the pre-Second World War period, the markets of East Asia – precisely because of the impoverishment produced by colonial exploitation – were too poor to attract significant investment, with the exception of Japan. The Philippines accounted for only 1.06 per cent of total US foreign investment; and the share for the Far East as a whole came to only 6 per cent.[3]

American domination of the Philippine economy was facilitated by the economic co-optation of the Philippine elite. Filipino landlords specializing in export crops like sugar benefited from free access to the US market, while landlords in heavily tenanted rice-and-corn lands were won over by the colonial administration's decision to respect existing property rights and not impose land reform. Rising land values, peasant indebtedness, landgrabbing opportunities afforded by the colonial administration's introduction of cadastral surveys and Torrens titles led to a strengthening of landlord power and a sharp increase in the proportion of the rural population classified as tenants and landless workers.

Just as in the Dutch East Indies, British Malaya and Japanese-dominated Korea, colonialism in the Philippines brought economic benefits to an elite composed of colonial traders and investors and the local gentry. For the vast majority of Filipinos, however, colonialism was an economic disaster, a fact underlined by the escalation of agrarian unrest in the 1930s.

Export-oriented Industrialization (EOI)

The immediate postwar period saw little change in the pattern of US investment in East Asia, which was focused on the production of agricultural commodities and the extraction of raw materials for export. This concentration on agriculture and extractive activities was encouraged by Washington, which worried about the dependence of the US economy on Southeast Asia's raw materials. As Assistant Secretary of State Dean Rusk put it in 1951, 'Our vital dependence upon Southeast Asia for tin is almost as great as for rubber.'[4] Control over Southeast Asia's resources by US and western business interests was also crucial for broader strategic reasons: it would deny them to the Soviets, thus preventing a change in the international balance of forces that favored the west.[5]

Some investment did go to manufacturing subsidiaries producing for local markets, a move that was necessitated by the high tariffs and quantitative restrictions on imported manufactures imposed by Third World governments that saw protected markets as the key to domestic industrialization. But given the small size of markets constrained by poverty and underdevelopment, manufacturing investment of this kind was relatively small.

In the 1960s and 1970s, however, a quantitative and qualitative shift occurred in US investment patterns in East Asia. An increasingly significant share of investment was devoted to export manufacturing. This trend stemmed from the conjunction of two factors: the emerging development strategy proposed by the World Bank and intensified competition among multinational firms.

As Third World 'development' came into vogue in the 1960s, technocrats at the US Agency for International Development and the US-dominated World Bank told Third World countries that the route to development did not lie in protected markets, as economic nationalists claimed. Industrialization via 'import substitution' would be easily exhausted, the Bank technocrats contended, because there was limited effective demand as a result of poverty and inequality.

Third World countries should instead employ their reserves of plentiful and cheap labor to turn out low-tech manufactures like textiles, garments and shoes for export to advanced country markets where their low labor costs would give them a competitive advantage. As World Bank president Robert McNamara put it in 1975, 'special efforts must be made in many countries to turn their manufacturing enterprises from the relatively small markets associated with import substitution toward the much larger opportunities flowing from export promotion.'[6]

The World Bank's prescription of what came to be known as export-oriented industrialization, or EOI, coincided, perhaps not coincidentally, with the needs of US multinational enterprises in the late 1960s and early 1970s. With competition intensifying among them and between them and the Japanese, US multinationals saw the reduction of their labor costs as the key to profitability. The relatively high wages of unionized US labor were seen as the problem, and the low wages of ununionized East Asian and Mexican labor provided the solution. The disparity in the cost of labor was revealed by the following figures for the early 1970s: while average monthly earnings of a US worker stood at about $1220 in 1972, workers made an average of only $45 in Taiwan, $68 in South Korea, $60 in Singapore and $82 in Hong Kong.

From 1965 to 1980, private US investment abroad rose fourfold, from $50 billion to $214 billion.[7] By 1988, over $32 billion dollars' worth of US investment was located in the Asia-Pacific. In manufacturing, exports accounted for 40 per cent of the sales of US overseas affiliates.[8] Indeed, an increasingly significant portion of the sales of US affiliates in the Asia-Pacific was exported to the US market, with the figure rising from less than 10 per cent in 1966 to more than 25 per cent in 1977.[9]

The obverse of growing manufacturing investment in East Asia was the 'hollowing out' of US industry. This was shown in the dynamics of the television industry. In the effort to compete with cheap but high-quality Japanese television sets flooding the US market, American firms moved many of their operations to Mexico, Taiwan and later Singapore in the 1960s. By the mid-1970s, although some 20 per cent of the black-and-white receivers sold in the US were still nominally produced there, 'substantial imports of subassemblies and parts from locations in Mexico and Taiwan were incorporated into these sets'.[10] In the case of the color television industry, the emigration to Mexico and East Asia of key manufacturing operations resulted in the value of overseas-produced subassemblies and parts rising from 23 per cent to more than 90 per cent of total components used by US firms.[11] During this period, jobs in the US television manufacturing industry fell 50 per cent between 1966 and 1970, and by another 30 per cent between 1971 and 1975.[12]

Promoting the 're-export' phenomenon, whereby US produced components were sent back to the US in the form of finished products assembled by cheap foreign labor was US trade policy: sections 806 and 807 of the US tariff code provided for the duty-free entry of the US components of imported manufactures, which meant that only the value added by assembly work was taxed. The value of '806/807' imports went from $953 million in 1966 to almost $40 billion in 1987.[13]

The competitive dynamics of the move to East Asia and Southeast Asia were evident in the fact that the relocation of many of the operations of the US television manufacturing industry to Taiwan provoked the Japanese producers also to transfer their labor-intensive operations to Taiwan and South Korea to overcome the temporary American advantage in labor costs. This process of trying to undercut each other by moving to low-wage East Asian and Southeast Asian sites was paralleled by US and Japanese firms in the microchip and computer industries.

The 'East Asia Edge', to use a popular image, was nowhere more evident than in the greater profitability of US investment there relative to other regions. While the rate of return on US investment in 1984 was 4.3 in Europe and 7.2 in Latin America, the figure for Asia was 14.0. Among individual Asian countries, the rate of return was much higher: 21.8 for Taiwan, 34.7 for Singapore and 41.2 for South Korea.[14]

Direct investment in East Asia was just one route by which American corporations could take advantage of the cheap labor resources of the area. Instead of investing directly, some multinationals preferred to enter into 'subcontracting' or OEM ('original equipment manufacturer') arrangements with local firms to manufacture products which would then be sold under their brand names. Taiwan, in particular, became a subcontracting center, with small Taiwanese firms producing for US firms such as K Mart, Sears, J.C. Penney, Hewlett-Packard, Texas Instruments, IBM, Schwinn Bicycle Company and General Electric, Taiwan's biggest 'exporter'. Subcontracting became so institutionalized that one foreign executive remarked, 'You really can't consider Taiwan an exporting nation. Taiwan is simply a collection of international subcontractors for the American market.'[15]

These ideal conditions for multinationals did not evolve naturally. They were created by governments eager to attract foreign investment at any cost. Among the more attractive investment come-on's were the so-called 'Export Processing Zones' (EPZs), such as those established in Bataan in the Philippines, Kaohsiung in Taiwan and Masan in South Korea. Firms settling in such zones were awarded a package of incentives like the one offered by the Bataan EPZ in the Philippines, which included: permission for 100 per cent foreign ownership; permission to impose a minimum wage lower than in Manila, the capital city; tax-exemption privileges, including tax credits on domestic capital equipment, tax exemptions on imported raw materials and equipment, exemption from the export tax and from municipal and provincial taxes; preferential access to Central Bank foreign exchange allocations for imports; low rents for land and water; government financing of infrastructure and factory buildings, which could then be rented or purchased by companies at a low price; and accelerated depreciation of fixed assets.

But perhaps the key contribution made by East Asian governments to the creation of an attractive climate for foreign investors was the repressive control of the working class, which drove the wages of workers below the market value of their labor.

Labor Control: the Korean Model

While labor was tightly controlled throughout East Asia, it was perhaps in South Korea that the harshest as well as the most sophisticated mechanisms of labor control were developed to promote EOI.

In the effort to demobilize labor systematically, the South Korean military government constructed three lines of containment: legal, ideological and repressive. All three were drawn to form a nearly impenetrable mesh during the 17-year rule of Park Chung-Hee, from 1962 to 1979.

A series of laws was passed which virtually outlawed strikes and banned independent trade unionism. But Korea's military rulers were sensitive to the fact that labor control based only on legal dicta or force would be highly unstable. Thus efforts were also expended to formulate and institutionalize mechanisms for the ideological containment of the workers. Perhaps the most important of these efforts was the Factory *Saemaul* (New Community) Movement, which sought to put labor on an ideological 'war footing' against the 'communist enemy' to achieve production objectives. On the one hand, Factory Saemaul attempted to exploit the traditional high value placed on collectivism and patriotism to achieve economic targets set by the state and management. On the other, Factory Saemaul work teams, which operated on such principles as 'work hard without being conscious of the closing hour of work' and 'workers should behave towards employers as sons to their fathers', were actually a means to subvert unions and, in many cases, to militarize the factory atmosphere.

But neither laws nor ideological co-optation could replace force and repression as the prime instrument for keeping the Korean working class in its place in the program of cheap-labor-dependent export-oriented growth. Indeed, one of the distinctive features of the Korean state is that the evolution of the internal security apparatus was greatly determined by the need to monitor and repress labor as part of a broader economic strategy. In Park's economic development program, noted one analyst, the Korean Central Intelligence Agency (KCIA) played a central role in separating 'the planning and implementation processes from any external political influences and controls, thereby minimizing "distortion" and "irrationality." It explains why the EPB [Economic Planning Board] and the intelligence agency possess a close relationship.'[16]

The KCIA labor-control program involved not only infiltrating factories with hundreds of agents but also making the government-controlled union leadership an adjutant of the state. This meant, above all, having a pliable set of officers for the nationwide Federation of Korean Trade Unions and key national unions like the Chemical Workers' Union. KCIA agents attended meetings of the central committees of the national unions and regularly intervened in elections to get candidates of their choice elected. Even though close government surveillance did not necessarily ensure that every election had the appropriate outcome, it meant that no uncooperative leader could win election at the national level.

But the ferment of dissent could not be contained by intimidation and manipulation, and the Korean military-technocrat alliance ultimately had to resort to the large-scale imprisonment, torture and assassination of workers in the increasingly more difficult effort to impose its strategy of development on a recalcitrant society.

Women Workers on the Cutting Edge

The phase of EOI that began in the 1960s was marked by the entry of women in large numbers into the manufacturing labor force throughout East and Southeast Asia. Export processing zones, in particular, were characterized by a predominantly female labor force, with the percentage of women reaching as high as 85 per cent of the work force in Taiwan's three EPZs.

The key reason was simple: for both foreign investors and local sub-contractors, women could be hired at wages lower than those for men. In Taiwan, for instance, during the 'take-off' years of the early 1970s, the average female wage was 62 per cent of the average male wage. Indeed, wage inequality was formalized in the Taiwan EPZs, with the salaries of women fixed at 10 to 20 per cent lower than the salaries of men workers doing comparable work.[17]

But there were other reasons articulated by male managers. As one personnel officer of an electronics assembly plant at the Kaohsiung EPZ commented, 'This job was done by boys two or three years ago. But we found that girls do the job as well and don't make trouble like the boys. They're obedient and pay attention to orders. So our policy is to hire all girls.'[18] Other zone managers alleged that men 'lack the manual dexterity of women, and are often a source of trouble at the factory'.[19]

In EPZs, control of the female work force extended beyond the workplace. Housed in barracks – euphemistically called 'dormitories' – that reminded visitors of '19th-century Manchester', women often found their dormitory lives totally controlled. As one account of dormitory life in Korea described it, 'The dormitory functioned as a mechanism by which workers' lives at work and off work were integrated and thus, employers could maximize their control over workers. Roommate shifts were frequently undertaken so that formation of social ties was minimized.'[20]

With the influx of women into manufacturing industries, a system of production evolved in which a male managerial hierarchy and white-collar aristocracy lorded it over a female blue-collar work force. Indeed, aside from receiving higher wages, male blue-collar workers enjoyed more job stability, engaged less in labor-intensive operations, had more freedom from overseers' interference, and were more easily co-opted by employers.[21]

Not surprisingly, these gender-based differences in power and privilege at the workplace were often translated into sexual harassment and sexual exploitation. As one observer of life at Kaohsiung recounted, 'every evening foremen and managers at the EPZ, along with many shopkeepers and businessmen from town ... drive up to the dorms in cars and motorcycles and pick up a bored, lonely, and overworked woman for an evening of pleasure.'[22] In the late 1970s, alongside photography shops and pharmacies across the street from the women's dormitory at Kaohsiung were abortion clinics – grim reminders of what passed for social life at the EPZ.

But managers expecting docility from women sometimes were in for a rude shock. In the Philippines, women workers at the Bataan EPZ became key elements in the ferment of labor organizing that helped bring down the Marcos dictatorship. In Singapore, women workers from neighboring Malaysia braved the wrath of one of the most effective labor-control regimes in Southeast Asia in May 1973 by striking against a US-owned plastics company and marching to the US Embassy with posters urging Americans to 'go home to your villages'.[23] The strike leaders were quickly deported by the Lee Kuan-Yew government.

But it was in Korea that women so emphatically proved the stereotype of docility wrong. There, underpaid female workers in the textile and garment industries spearheaded the drive for labor rights with demonstrations, sit-ins and hunger strikes. A sense of the heroic character of these struggles is communicated by the strike of women workers against the Dong-Il Textile Company, which was marked by 'sit-in demonstrations, the workers' fast at Myungdong Cathedral, a demonstration by about 70 women workers who stood nude, forming a human wall in front of riot police, an attack by male workers on women workers by throwing human excrement over them, mass dismissal, and detentions'.[24] Summing up labor organizing in the 1970s, labor expert Choi Jang-Jip claims, 'the women workers have really been the driving force not only to bestow on the nascent labor movement a dynamic character but also to actually lead it at a grassroots level.'[25]

Economic Growth and Income Concentration

The gross domestic product of the Asia-Pacific region grew by 6 per cent per annum in the period from 1960 to 1982, and by 8 per cent per year between 1982 and 1987.[26] This impressive growth must, however, be balanced against the tremendous political, social and environmental costs it incurred.

Denial of democratic rights by authoritarian regimes was the norm for much of the 'growth' period from 1965 to 1990 in the region's key economies: Taiwan, South Korea, the Philippines, Singapore, Indonesia, Thailand, Malaysia and China.

And in many countries, conditions of economic existence have worsened for the majority. In the Philippines, the number of families living under the poverty line rose from less than 50 per cent in 1971 to 70 per cent by 1986. Even in the model NICs ('newly industrializing countries'), Taiwan and South Korea, rapid economic growth has gone hand-in-hand with the intensification of inequality. In South Korea, during the crucial 20-year period between 1965 and 1985, the share of income going to the bottom 40 per cent of the population declined from 19.3 per cent to 17.7 per cent, while the share going to the top 20 per cent rose from 41.8 per cent to 43.7 per cent.[27] In Taiwan, the share of the income going to the bottom 40 per cent dropped from 22.6 per cent in 1978 to 21.8 per cent in 1986, while the top 20 per cent raised their share from 37.1 per cent of income to 38.2 per cent.[28]

In both Taiwan and South Korea, the increasing concentration of wealth at the top was manifested in a crisis of housing. In Korea, 65.2 per cent of all private landholdings nationwide were concentrated in the hands of 5 per cent of the population. The other face of this phenomenon was a rise in the number of renters, squatters and homeless, from 50 per cent of the residents of Seoul in 1970 to 60 per cent by 1985.[29] In Taiwan, where five billionaires had more net wealth than 11 billionaires in Japan, home ownership was beyond the reach of an estimated 21 per cent of the population.[30]

In Thailand, now labeled the 'fifth Asian dragon', after Taiwan, South Korea, Singapore and Hong Kong, the economy grew by 8 per cent in the late 1980s and by 10 per cent in 1990. This growth, however, was accompanied by an appalling concentration of income: the top 20 per cent of the population increased its share of the national income from 49.8 per cent in 1962 to 55.6 per cent in 1986. At the same time, the bottom 20 per cent saw its share decline from 8.0 per cent to 4.6 per cent.[31] Among the realities expressed by these statistics are rising rural poverty, with 85 per cent of villages now facing bankruptcy, and some 800000 women, most of them from impoverished rural areas, earning a living as prostitutes.

EOI and the Destruction of Agriculture

The impoverishment of the rural sector in Thailand is a repetition of the experience of South Korea and Taiwan, where agriculture is today in a nearly terminal state. This is hardly surprising since the Korean and Taiwanese technocrats deliberately subordinated agriculture to the interests of export manufacturers. By holding down the price of agricultural commodities, the price of urban labor would be kept low, resulting in cheap, competitive exports. As one analyst put it, 'Low grain price policies were adopted as a means of surplus extraction ... The state was, in effect, engaged in forming an export-oriented entrepreneurial class that was competitive in world markets. Keeping wage costs low facilitated this ... strategy.'[32]

During the early phase of EOI in Korea, farm household income plunged from parity with urban household income to 67 per cent of the latter in just five years, 1965 to 1970. With farming becoming unprofitable, a process of uncontrolled urbanization took place. In Korea, the percentage of the population living in rural areas dropped from 56 per cent in 1966 to 17 per cent in 1988. This was a precipitous drop not only in relative terms but in absolute terms as well, from 15.8 million to 7.8 million. The rate of migration was one of the highest in the world, approaching an average of 400000 yearly in the mid-1980s. Since the vast majority of migrants have been young men and women, their departure has resulted in a rapidly ageing work force: the portion of the agricultural work force aged 50 and over shot up from 19 per cent in the early 1980s to almost 33 per cent by the end of 1988.

The same dislocation occurred in Taiwan, with the one difference that population transfer was more consciously part of government strategy than in South Korea. Lee Teng-Hui, who was an agricultural technocrat before he became president of Taiwan, admitted, 'The government has intentionally held down peasants' income so as to transfer these people – who were formerly engaged in agriculture – into industries.'[33]

The second phase of EOI's destructive impact on agriculture was the application of green revolution technology – chemical-intensive agriculture – to raise productivity and lower food costs in order to maintain the low cost of labor. Higher production was achieved, but at a tremendous cost to farmers: they were driven to deep indebtedness by the costly fertilizer and pesticide inputs that accompanied green revolution technology. While farm income and assets in Korea rose three times between 1975 and 1980, debt increased *10* times. The number of rural households in debt rose from 76 per cent in 1971, to 90 per cent in 1983, to an astounding 98 per cent in 1985. By 1988, close to 20 per cent of total farm debt was incurred to make payments on past debt, leading one observer to note that 'farmers are trapped in a vicious cycle in which they repeatedly pull out the bottom rock and stack it atop the top rock.'[34]

Today, agriculture in Taiwan and Korea may be entering its terminal phase, many observers fear. Under pressure from the United States, mechanisms protecting beef, poultry, vegetable, tobaccco and even the once-sacrosanct commodity, rice, are either in the process of being dismantled or in grave danger of being removed to make these economies a dumping ground for American agricultural production. This is the *quid pro quo* needed to keep US markets open to manufactured goods from Taiwan and Korea. For nearly 30 years, agriculture had been subordinated to industry, with disastrous consequences. Now, Taiwanese and Korean farmers complain bitterly, food security is about to be thrown to the winds as the technocrats prepare to offer agriculture as the 'sacrificial lamb' to save export manufacturing interests.

EOI and Political Instability

Apart from collapsing agricultural sectors, another byproduct of EOI has been political instability. This is related to the repression that marked the first phases of industrialization. That repression was justified by authoritarian elites with such slogans as 'growth first, democracy later.' In their view, which was shared by many western political analysts, the material conditions for democracy would be laid by authoritarian regimes, leading to a stable transition from authoritarianism to democracy once prosperity became universal.

Developments in South Korea and Taiwan, however, did not conform to this ideal transition. Instead, they seemed to indicate that one of the harvests of labor-repressive export-oriented industrialization was permanent social and political instability. In Korea, the repressed political energy of three decades of labor repression broke out in over 7000 strikes between 1987 and 1980, bringing an end to, among other things, the myth of the 'Confucian worker' laboring 12 hours a day out of respect for his employer. It revealed, instead, a bitter social divide between those who had benefited from export-oriented growth and those who felt exploited by it. The social legacy of high-speed export-oriented growth was an extremely class-conscious labor force that had little common ground with management, making it difficult for either western-style collective bargaining or Japanese-style company unionism to be institutionalized.

In both Korea and Taiwan, workers, allied with disaffected sectors of the middle class, led the drive for democracy against recalcitrant political and economic elites. But given the deep divide created by EOI, democratization in both societies did not lead to a peaceable process of compromise over economic and social issues, but to a polarized struggle over the benefits of past economic growth. As the UK's *Financial Times* commented, in respect of Korea, 'the country's new-found democratic politics are putting wage-push, labor unrest, and demands for welfare expenditure in the way of continued super-growth.'[35]

The labor repression that was central to successful export-oriented growth, in short, had precluded the possibility of stable democratization. Instead, it had created societies where class conflict was endemic and political legitimacy was precarious. From the point of view of the working class, despite the fact that EOI had brought high growth rates, it was stamped with a fundamental illegitimacy. This perspective was expressed most cogently by Lee So-Sun, one of Korea's most respected labor leaders, when asked if strikes by Korean workers were undermining the competitiveness of Korea's exports. 'The government says the economy is successful', she replied angrily. 'But only a few benefit from the economy ... There is nothing in it for us.'[36]

Conclusion

In the last few decades, the traditional mode of colonial exploitation, which focused on the extraction of natural resources, has been gradually superseded by a process of export-oriented industrialization. This phenomenon cannot be divorced from the growing demand for cheap industrial labor by US and Japanese firms and the policies of labor repression enacted by East Asian states to attract foreign capital. While it has brought relatively high growth rates to a number of economies, EOI has also reaped major social and economic costs, among them increasing inequality, the destruction of agriculture and the alienation of labor. The repression of labor that went with EOI also guaranteed that the process of democratization, when it came, would lead, not to a peaceable compromise on economic and social issues, but to a polarized struggle over the benefits of past growth, and a political system marked by long-term instability.

7

Ecological Disequilibrium

Among the most alarming byproducts of export-oriented economic development has been the degradation of the environment. In fact, 'disaster' is now the word that comes to the lips of those who survey the state of the environment in the Asia-Pacific region.

Destroying the Rainforests

The unremitting destruction of tropical rainforests is perhaps the dimension of the environmental crisis that is most publicized. This phenomenon is directly associated with the colonial pattern of resource extraction for export to the advanced economies that was carried over to the post-colonial period. The scale of destruction is unparalleled, as the following brief survey reveals:

From over 50 per cent in 1950, the portion of the Philippines covered by forests dropped to less than 25 per cent by 1990. Seventy per cent of Thailand was virgin forest in 1932; by 1990, only 17 per cent of the nation was forested. In the Malaysian state of Sarawak, loggers eliminated 30 per cent of the forest area in barely 23 years, 1962 to 1985; unless stopped, they will eliminate the rest by the year 2000. And in just eight years, 1982 to 1990, a third of the forests of the island of Sumatra, in Indonesia, have disappeared.[1]

With the depletion of forest resources in Thailand, the Philippines and Malaysia, loggers are now moving in force to Burma (Myanma), which contains 80 per cent of the world's remaining teak stock, and to the countries of Indochina. According to the International Burma Campaign,

> [T]he last of the world's great teak forests is being devastated at a horrifying rate, with replanting almost nil. Burma now has the third highest deforestation rate on the planet, with 1.2 million acres of its tree cover disappearing each year. If the rate is not curtailed, Burma will be virtually denuded in fifteen years, with rainforests along the Thai-Burma border gone in five years. Thailand's soldier businessmen may not be entirely joking when they reportedly propose toasts to the 'last tree in Burma.'[2]

Hungry for foreign exchange, Vietnamese enterprises have been making deals with wood-hungry Japanese conglomerates to sell both Cambodian wood and their own. With half of Vietnam's forest cover already lost to American defoliation during the Vietnam War, the government has recently allowed state enterprises and private firms to triple timber production in the Central Highlands, where there are already 2.3 million acres of bare hillside.[3] In Cambodia, joint ventures between the Phnom Penh government and the Vietnamese are paralleled by logging deals between the Khmer Rouge and Thai companies, creating a deadly combination that has reduced the country's forest cover from 13 million hectares to 7 million hectares, according to an official estimate.[4] In neighboring Laos, forest cover is being reduced at the rate of 500000 acres a day, leading to projections that only 26 per cent of the country's forests will be left by the year 2000. As in Burma and Vietnam, a major cause is unrestrained activity by logging interests, which export about 30 to 40 per cent of wood that is legally cut and a substantial volume of illegally logged timber.[5]

The loss of the forests has reduced biodiversity by condemning many plant and animal species to extinction. This has detrimental consequences on, among other things, medical research, since 25 per cent of the world's pharmaceutical products are derived from tropical plants.[6] When combined with poaching and officially sanctioned trade, the destruction of forest habitat has led to the rapid loss of wildlife. In Burma, for instance, endangered species include the Asian elephant, clouded leopard, musk deer, gaur, Malayan tapir, Fea's Muntjac, and silver leaf monkey.[7] Deforestation has also been accompanied by ethnocide, as forest peoples are dispersed, displaced or simply murdered by logging firms and slash-and-burn small cultivators that follow in the wake of the big loggers. The Kayan and Penan in Sarawak, the Karen and Karenni in Burma, the Batak, Aeta and Agta in the Philippines are all peoples who face the same threat of extinction in the short term.

Floods stemming from deforestation are now a common occurrence throughout Southeast Asia. In Thailand, indiscriminate logging led to disaster in November 1988, when floods and landslides ravaged 116 districts, destroyed 16000 homes, damaged 1 million acres of farmland and killed close to 400 people. An even bigger catastrophe was visited on the Philippines when heavy rains and deforestation combined to create a massive mudslide that killed 8000 people in the city of Ormoc, many of them swept out to sea where they were eaten by sharks. Commenting on the disaster, Yoichi Kuroda, head of the Japan Tropical Action Network (JATAN), claimed, '70 per cent of the timber logged in the Philippines went to Japan, and logging was the cause of the disaster.'[8]

Once stripped of their forest cover, tropical lands become very vulnerable to erosion. In the northeast of Thailand, one study revealed that out of 106 million *rai* (about 53 million acres), close to half, or about 43 million *rai*, were eroded.[9] In the Philippines, it is estimated that over 22.5 million acres – or more than half of the land area in 21 provinces – are afflicted with erosion.[10]

The US and Export-oriented Forestry

While deforestation is often attributed to local loggers, slash-and-burn farmers and governments, it is important to underline that the basic pattern of rapid exploitation for export was set by colonial powers and continues to be sustained by foreign demand and to be supported by western development agencies.

In the Philippines, for instance, the voracious US demand for wood placed the 'modernization' of the logging industry among the top priorities of the colonial administration that took over the country at the turn of the century. As Richard Tucker notes,

> From the Forest Law of 1904 onwards, US colonial policy set about to modernize the logging industry as rapidly as possible, through close cooperation between the Bureau of Forestry and large-scale timber corporations, both foreign and domestic. Philippine logging came to be dominated by a capital-intensive, technologically modern sector. Great profits accrued to the major investors, but the rainforests of the islands were depleted at an increasing rate by the allure of international markets.[11]

A close working relationship between the Bureau of Forestry and American firms, which accounted for 42 per cent of investment in the nation's sawmill industry by the end of the colonial period in 1941, transformed the Philippines from a timber importer into Southeast Asia's largest timber exporter.[12] Philippine dipterocarps, particularly mahogany, found their way to many markets, but the biggest single market was the United States. The colonial authorities led the export drive, with Bureau of Forestry promotional booklets reminding US customers that 'When you buy Philippine lumber, you are helping not only the Filipinos, but also the American lumbermen in the Philippines and the American machine manufacturers in the United States.'[13]

Though Filipino lumbermen began to dominate the industry after independence in 1946, the pattern of massive exporting had been set, and the Philippines continued to be the region's top timber exporter in the 1950s and 1960s. By then the country's forest cover had declined to less than 50 per cent. The impact of American policy was described by a leading American forester after a 1959 tour of the country's forest lands:

> Some weeks ago I visited Cebu, Bohol and Negros. Parts of these islands made me think I was back again in Korea, North China, or the man-made deserts of Mexico. For I saw thousands upon thousands of hectares of cut-over, burned-over and abandoned land, pock-marked with red and yellow scars of bare earth at the mercy of sun, wind, and rain.[14]

By the 1960s, Japan replaced the United States as the main market for Philippine forest products, accounting for as much as 70 per cent of timber logged up to the 1990s, according to some estimates.[15] It is important to note, however, that Japan, which is now the world's main consumer of tropical forest products, was stepping into the roles of unrestrained consumer and ecologically insensitive investor that had been pioneered by the US.

The World Bank and Deforestation

The World Bank, the US-dominated multilateral development agency, has played a significant role in the deforestation and consequent ecological degradation of Southeast Asia and the Pacific.

One of the most notorious instances of World Bank participation in environmental destruction was its funding of Indonesia's Transmigration Program to the tune of $600 million between 1976 and 1986. The program, which involved resettling millions of people from crowded Java on the outer islands, resulted in ecological disruption in Sulawesi, Sumatra and Irian Jaya. Some 30 per cent of Sulawesi's land was converted from forest to resettlement sites. The loss of the fragile forest ecosystem, however, degraded the soil to the point where it could not sustain subsistence agriculture or even simply absorb water. In Sumatra, some 2.3 million hectares of land formerly covered by forest declined to the same degraded state. In Irian Jaya, ethnocide accompanied deforestation as the traditional Melanesian communities that resisted the settler onslaught were subjected to violent responses, like bombing and burning of their villages by the Indonesian armed forces, which are not known for their finesse in these matters.[16]

In Thailand, a World Bank-supported program contributed to the November 1988 flash floods, which wreaked havoc on the southern part of the country. A government agency investigating the disaster pointed to the rapid expansion of rubber plantations in the area, an activity that was designed and financed by the Bank. This process involved cutting down old, mature rubber trees and replacing them with new clonal varieties. The loss of the old rubber trees under this so-called 'rubber replanting program' led to severe soil erosion and eventually the tragic floods.[17]

Perhaps the most direct link between Bank policy and deforestation is provided by the experience of Papua New Guinea (PNG). In 1964, a World Bank mission to that country recommended an 'aggressive policy of commercial development' of the forest industry.[18] According to David Lamb,

> [The Bank] argued that PNG's timber resources were large and could therefore be more heavily utilized to finance the country's development. In the Bank's view the existing mills were mostly too small and under-capitalized, so it recommended trying to attract larger international companies with the managerial, financial and marketing skills necessary to build an export industry. These larger companies would, of course, require access to much greater forest concessions.[19]

The Australian government which then governed Papua New Guinea accepted this recommendation and proceeded to approach investors to develop that country's forest resources. In 1971, an agreement was reached with a Japanese firm, Honshu Paper Manufacturing, which gave the latter rights to harvest pulp and logs from 88000 hectares of forest near Madang on the north coast of the island. This contract was respected by the newly independent Papua New Guinean government which assumed power in 1973.

After 20 years, the operation has resulted in 'massive environmental damage', according to a parliamentary representative from Madang Province – a conclusion supported by the forestry department. The Honshu subsidiary felled 60000 hectares of virgin tropical forest to make 'cardboard boxes for stereos and televisions',[20] but it had shirked the responsibility for reforesting the area, thus violating the terms of its logging permit. Moreover, according to an official inquiry, the company had used 'creative accounting to avoid clearing of profit in Papua New Guinea for 17 years, thereby avoiding paying royalties and taxes to the people and the government'.[21]

While the Japanese company was cast in the role of the villain, responsibility for the disaster was clearly shared by the World Bank which had set the stage for the tragedy with its recommendation of aggressive development of export-oriented forestry with little regard for the environmental impact of such a strategy.

The World Bank and the 'Big Dam Syndrome'

The World Bank has been accused of promoting not only inappropriate forestry policies but also ecologically and socially disruptive energy and irrigation programs. Indeed, the Bank has been the main agent for the introduction of the gigantic energy-generation, centralized electrification and centralized irrigation technologies pioneered in the US in such projects as the Tennessee Valley Authority and the Grand Coulee Dam.

Applied to the traditional agricultural systems of Asia and the Pacific, the savings represented by 'economies of scale' have been offset by social costs of forced resettlement of hundreds of thousands of people and the negative environmental impact on local ecosystems.

During the Marcos dictatorship, for instance, a Bank feasibility study recommended the development of the Philippines' most ambitious hydroelectric project: a gigantic four-dam complex to harness the power of the Chico River in the highlands of northern Luzon to serve the needs of distant Manila and its multinational firms. In the process, 100000 tribal people would have had to be relocated from their ancestral lands. Fortunately, the project did not materialize, but this was only after fierce resistance from the Kalinga and Bontoc peoples.[22]

The Bank was more successful in Indonesia. In central Java, it contributed 80 per cent of the costs of the Kedung Ombo Dam, which involved the displacement of 20000 people for the sake of 'development'. Villagers targeted for displacement have protested against the grossly inadequate resettlement and compensation schemes and the Indonesian authorities' resorting to coercion and intimidation, with about 5000 people refusing to budge despite the reservoir's being filled up in 1990.[23]

In Thailand, up to 20000 people face forced resettlement from the construction of the Pak Mun Hydroelectric Dam, which is awaiting Bank funding after the Bank approved inadequate resettlement plans and questionable environmental impact assessments. The Mun is the most important tributary of the Mekong River, containing 100 species of fish and a rich assortment of riverine fauna on which hundreds of thousands depend for their food and income. The Bank assessment did not include studies on fish migratory patterns and acknowledged that the worst-case scenario would be 'a major impact on the fish population of both river systems'.[24]

The combined environmental and social impact of Kedung Ombo and Pak Mun, however, would be dwarfed by that of the Three Gorges Dam planned for the Yangtze River, a project with which the Bank has been involved since 1986. Billed as the world's biggest hydro-electric dam, it would also involve one of the world's largest forced resettlement schemes, with up to 1.2 million farmers, fishermen and urban dwellers likely to see their homes submerged by the 600-kilometer-long dam.[25] Indeed, the Bank claims that 'there should be no question that the resettlement of about 700000 people will be a difficult task under the best of circumstances.'[26] The Bank has endorsed an expert review favoring implementation of the project and 'has reserved any decision to help in the execution of the project, should the Government decide to proceed and should it request the Bank's assistance'.[27]

Depletion of Fisheries and Coastal Resources

Deforestation and disruption of riverine ecosystems by the big dam syndrome have been paralleled by the depletion of the region's fishing and coastal resources. Overfishing by Japanese, American, Korean and Taiwanese trawlers, many of them using the murderously efficient 'driftnet' technique, has destroyed traditionally rich fishing grounds throughout the Pacific, leaving local fishermen with less sophisticated methods to compete destructively for the smaller stocks of fish.

Once regarded as a mechanism that could reverse the effects of commercial fishing, Exclusive Economic Zones (EEZs) of 200 miles established by the Law of the Sea have been hijacked by the logic of export-oriented growth. As one expert sees it,

[T]he valuable species such as tuna and mackerel are already fished by distant-water fishing countries, and some national development policies view joint ventures with foreign companies as vehicles for technically modern exploitation, processing, and marketing of these resources. Thus high-value fish are exported out of the region to developed countries while intraregional, offshore and artisanal fishermen compete with each other for dwindling coastal resources, sometimes violently.[28]

In the competition for reduced coastal fish stocks, smaller fishermen have resorted to dynamite fishing, cyanide fishing, and *muro-ami* (noise/netting) methods, which not only capture excessive numbers of fish but also destroy coral reefs. Damaged both by fishing and water pollution, less than 6 per cent of the coral cover of the Philippines' coastal resources remains in excellent condition.[29]

The supply of fish has also been reduced by the destruction of mangroves, their coastal breeding grounds, as more and more of these are converted into fish or prawn farms servicing mainly export markets. In the Philippines, a recent satellite study revealed that of the 500000 hectares of original mangrove species vegetation in the 1920s, only 38000 hectares remain.[30]

The Costs of Chemical-intensive Agriculture

Over the last three decades, genetic manipulation through advanced breeding techniques has transformed agricultural technology in the Asia-Pacific. The so-called 'green revolution' started at the Rockefeller Foundation-financed International Rice Research Institute (IRRI) in the Philippine town of Los Banos and was promoted throughout Asia by the World Bank, the US Agency for International Development and US agrochemical companies. Governments and farmers throughout Asia were encouraged to switch to a technology which promised not only self-sufficiency in rice production but also export capability.

The result was increased grain yields throughout East Asia, accompanied by reduced biodiversity, increased water pollution and a more risky working environment for farmers.

The promotion of a few 'high-yield' varieties (HYVs) of rice seed has resulted in the neglect and loss of scores of traditional varieties that adapted over time to their environment.[31] Biodiversity has also been reduced by the massive fertilizer and pesticide applications of green revolution technology: in Korea, to cite one example, over 110 species of flora and fauna are reported to have vanished as a result of indiscriminate fertilizer and pesticide use.[32]

Heavy use of nitrogen-source and other chemical fertilizers contributes to soil acidification, zinc losses and decline in soil fertility. Fertilizers and pesticides are a major source of contamination of surface water and groundwater, and pesticide overuse threatens the health of workers and consumers alike. In the Philippines, many cases of death and sterilization from pesticides have been reported. Paraquat poisoning, which has hit mainly Indian estate workers in Malaysia, appears to have reached 'unacceptable levels'.[33] In Taiwan, claims sociologist Michael Hsiao, 'There are many cases of sudden death among farmers, and this is often attributed to pesticides.'[34]

So great is the fear of pesticides among Taiwanese farmers – who use 1 per cent of the world's pesticide production – that a special class of hired laborers who are described as 'no good' men has emerged to carry out the task of spraying pesticides on crops.[35] The Taiwanese call this practice 'paying money and letting others die'.[36] Indeed, 'many farmers don't eat what they sell on the market', one expert claims. 'They grow another crop without using pesticides and that's what they consume.'[37] Some consumers, however, are not fooled. And increasingly one finds shoppers examining produce for insects or insect bites in the belief that these are signs that the vegetables are free of pesticide residues.[38]

While HYVs initially increased yields, their promise often was evanescent. They lacked the resistance to diseases that centuries had bred into the traditional rice varieties, and this led to crop failures in places like the Philippines, Malaysia and Thailand. For instance, in 1973–4, virtually the entire Philippine rice crop was devastated by the Tungro virus which ravaged the showcase seed IR-20 and allied modern HYVs of rice.[39]

Moreover, the massive chemical assault on ricefields that accompanied the switch to HYVs began to backfire as pests began to develop resistance to pesticides. For example, indiscriminate pesticide spraying in Malaysia's Cameron Highlands resulted in the diamond back moth developing resistance to organophosphates and carbamates. This biological response triggered a chemical counter-attack, illustrating the deadly dynamics of chemical-intensive agriculture: farmers resorted to smuggling in extremely toxic brands or 'cocktailed' various pesticides 'to boost their killing power'.[40]

Agriculture dependent on HYVs and chemical-intensive processes is nearing a crisis point in Asia, just as it is in the United States. This is not coincidental, for many of the same forces and interests that transformed American agriculture also put Asia on the chemical-intensive path. Indeed, what the landmark study by US National Academy of Sciences, *Alternative Agriculture*, described for American agriculture could also be said word-for-word of Asian agriculture:

Specialization and related production practices, such as extensive synthetic chemical fertilizer and pesticide use, are contributing to environmental and occupational health problems as well as potential public health problems. Insects, weeds, and pathogens continue to develop resistance to commonly used insecticides, herbicides, and fungicides. Insects and pathogens also continue to overcome inbred genetic resistance of plants. Nitrate, predominantly from fertilizers and animal manures, and several widely used pesticides have been found in surface water and groundwater, making agriculture the leading non-point source of water pollution in many states. The decreasing genetic diversity of many major US crops and livestock species ... increases the potential for sudden widespread economic losses from disease.[41]

Industrialization and Toxification

While the environmental threats stemming from the green revolution are now well known, those created by Asia's other 'revolution', export-oriented industrialization, are just beginning to generate concern.

Indeed, pesticides and fertilizers are only one source of agricultural contamination. Another increasingly important source is waterborne industrial waste. In Taiwan, 20 per cent of farmland, the government itself admits, is now polluted by industrial waste water. As a result, 30 per cent of the rice grown on the island, says Dr Edgar Lin, one of the island's leading environmentalists, is contaminated with heavy metals, including mercury, arsenic and cadmium.[42]

Unregulated dumping of industrial and toxic waste has also killed rivers, damaged coastal systems and poisoned aquifers. The lower reaches of virtually all of Taiwan's major rivers are severely polluted. Untreated sewage and industrial waste have combined to kill all of Metro Manila's water systems. In Thailand, Asia's fastest growing economy,

> pollution has already reached a crisis state. The lower part of Bangkok's Chao Praya River is seriously polluted by uncontrolled dumping of industrial and household waste. The river's upper reaches, which supply most of Bangkok's water, are increasingly affected by seepage of agricultural chemicals, and some analysts cite evidence that such chemicals have contributed to the decrease in marine life in the Gulf of Thailand.[43]

Asia's top NIC, South Korea, has its share of environmental horror stories, but perhaps no tale is more terrifying than the experience of the 10 million people who draw their supplies from the Nakdong River, which snakes down the Taegu-Pusan metropolitan area, Korea's second most important industrial complex. In April 1991, they were told by the government that the funny smell they had noticed in their tap water was caused by the surreptitious dumping of some 325 tons of waste phenol, a highly toxic, cancer-causing chemical, by a subsidiary of Doosan, a Korean conglomerate that has joint ventures with Coca Cola, Kentucky Fried Chicken and Nestlé. The dumping, they were also informed, had been going on for over five months.[44]

The 'Korean Miracle' has also made the sulfur dioxide content of Seoul's air one of the world's highest and caused close to 70 per cent of the rain falling on the city to be so acidic as to pose a hazard to human beings.[45] Seoul's air pollution is not unique in being a serious health hazard; asthma cases among Taiwanese children have quadrupled over the last 10 years, and, according to one account, 'children in Bangkok have among the highest levels of lead in their blood, largely attributable to air pollution.'[46]

Confronted with already serious environmental threats generated by high-speed growth, the peoples of Taiwan and Korea, as well as the people of Japan, also have to face the potentially massive health and environmental consequences of nuclear power plant disasters. In spite of over 190 accidents at the country's operating nuclear reactors, Korea's technocrats continue to cherish dreams of building 55 new nuclear plants by the year 2031.[47] In Taiwan, the government continues to try to push through with plans to build a fourth nuclear plant, disregarding accidents, problems with the disposal of low-level waste and the lack of any viable plans for the long-term storage of spent fuel.[48] With 39 nuclear plants in operation, 11 under construction and three in the design stage, Japan is practically a floating nuclear reactor. The potentially lethal consequences of nuclear power were underlined on 9 February 1991, when a malfunction at the Mihama plant caused one reactor to emit higher than normal radiation into the atmosphere and gave Japan its worst nuclear accident yet.[49]

The environmental crisis created by export-oriented industrialization in East Asia is not an accidental byproduct of development or one that can be attributed to lack of foresight. In many countries, laws and regulatory bodies are in place. But technocrats are reluctant to enforce laws, for fear of chasing away local and foreign investors, many of whom set up shop in the first place to take advantage of a lax environmental regime. For many technocrats, in fact, some environmental destruction is the unavoidable price of economic growth. 'Some', however, is a fairly elastic term. And when we are witnessing processes of high-speed export-oriented industrialization that telescope into a few decades transformations that took many more decades to transpire in the US and other industrial countries, then 'some' can be devastating. Massive ecological destabilization, people throughout the region are beginning to realize, is intrinsic to export-oriented industrialization.

Environmental Troubles and Threats to the Pacific Islands

Ecological disequilibrium is not limited to the Western Pacific Rim. Indeed, it is probably far more serious in the fragile ecosystems of the South Pacific, a fact recently underlined by growing awareness of the consequences of the 'Greenhouse Effect', a process of global warming produced principally by emission of carbon dioxide, sulfur dioxide and other gases by the industrial economies of the North. Over the next 50 years, mean sea levels are expected to rise by 20–150 centimeters, with tidal peaks and storm surges possibly raising sea levels by 5–8 meters. This places those countries consisting entirely of atolls – Kiribati, the Marshall Islands, Tuvalu and Tokelau – in a very precarious situation.[50] In fact, the danger to Tokelau, a dependency of New Zealand which lies north of Western Samoa, is so proximate that one high government official recently said that 'the next cyclone to hit the territory might force a decision on whether evacuation was necessary.'[51]

Prior to the nineteenth century, the long distances between islands produced stable ecosystems in which plants and animals lost the defense mechanisms that would have ensured their survival in a more competitive context. With western political colonization also came a biological colonization by more aggressive animal and plant species that came with ships and other means of transport. The fragile balance that had been established between indigenous peoples and indigenous fauna and flora snapped. Massive extinctions of Hawaiian bird species, for instance, were triggered by the introduction of rats, cats, dogs, mongooses and pigs, while in New Zealand, the extinction of many species of indigenous land birds was associated with the arrival of rats on the outer islands. Meanwhile, cattle, goats and other imported herbivores chewed many plant species to extinction, leading to erosion in certain areas.[52]

Human activities were, nevertheless, the main cause of species extinction. Especially noteworthy was deforestation and its associated destruction of island fauna. The ecological tragedy in Madang, Papua New Guinea, discussed earlier, merely reenacts a process that took place earlier in other Pacific islands. Jeremy Carew-Reid's tragic survey makes this clear:

On many Pacific Islands, only fragments of undisturbed rural areas remain. For example, in American Samoa, two-thirds of the lowland rain-forest has been destroyed. In many islands of Micronesia the situation is more serious. The forests of Pohnpei and

Yap are mostly disturbed, and in Truk, no undisturbed areas exist. Only scattered and inaccessible remnants remain on Guam and there are none remaining on the Marshall Islands ... Further south, in Niue, the original tropical rain-forest of tall trees with a relatively dense canopy, has been reduced to small remnants surrounded by large expanses of scrub and fernlands resulting from prolonged over-cropping and soil impoverishment.[53]

The destructive impact of new intrusive economic activity on a fragile ecosystem was recently brought home anew by the appeal launched to stop not only driftnet fishing but also 'longlining', a Japanese fishing technique to catch tuna. According to New Zealand environmentalists, bait attached to lines attracts birds, which then sink with the line. This has resulted in the killing of thousands of seabirds in New Zealand, Australian and Indian Ocean waters, including 50 per cent of the worldwide population of the wandering albatross.[54]

Commercial mining has also been a cause of serious ecological disruption. In New Caledonia, the destruction of scrubland involved in the opencast mining of nickel has caused 'extensive erosion which sterilizes portions of the lagoon'.[55] In Papua New Guinea, severe environmental degradation has been a byproduct of copper and gold mining operations in Bougainville, Ok Tedi and Bulolo. But it is perhaps in phosphate-rich Nauru that export-oriented mining has wrought the greatest havoc. Though the 8-square mile island has the highest GNP per capita in the Pacific ($20444), 80 per cent of its natural environment has been destroyed.[56] Moreover, traditional cultural patterns

... could not adapt to the sudden onset of affluence. The Nauru community has the highest per capita income in the South Pacific but also one of the highest levels of diabetes in the world, unusually high levels of alcoholism and cardiovascular disease and one of the lowest life expectancy rates in the region. These problems have meant that improved conditions of material living have been accompanied by a severe degradation in cultural and social values.[57]

The ecological tragedies spawned by mining are likely to increase as that sector has been designated as the 'growth industry' for some Pacific economies, like Papua New Guinea and the Solomon Islands, by the World Bank, the Australian government and foreign investors. For example, in the Solomon Islands, prospecting licenses have been issued to 15 mining companies and 84 applications are awaiting consideration.[58]

Water pollution from organic and industrial waste as a result of rising tourist and increasing manufacturing activity is also coming to the forefront as an environmental problem. Disposal of waste from the Cook Islands' juice cannery has led to decreased biodiversity in the harbor, while in the Solomon Islands, organic waste flowing from the palm oil processing plant has degraded the surrounding sea. In Fiji, untreated waste from tourist resorts is destroying coral communities. Fiji is also the center of export-oriented manufacturing in the region, with some 7000 enterprises in operation. According to a United Nations study of the environmental impact of these firms, 'in general, there is no real anti-pollution treatment by most firms' and 'small firms do not usually have measures regarding waste disposal'.[59]

Toxic pollution has emerged as a prominent hazard to both health and habitat. Pesticides are one source of the toxic threat: of the 620 pesticides imported for use in the region, 94 are classified as 'extremely or highly hazardous' by the World Health Organization (WHO), 99 are banned or severely restricted in the United States, and 177 are not registered for use in Australia and New Zealand.[60] While pesticide runoff from agricultural activities serves as the most common conduit of toxic chemicals to marine life and coral reefs, there are increasing instances of pesticides being used to kill fish, with toxic consequences for both lagoon ecosystems and the health of consumers. In Truk, for instance, pesticides were responsible for a fish kill that came to 20 tons.[61] Not surprisingly, serious multiple poisonings of consumers have been reported throughout Micronesia.[62]

The threat from toxic substances has now been magnified as western firms eye the South Pacific as disposal sites for large quantities of hazardous waste. Western Samoa, Tonga and Papua New Guinea have been among the countries approached by a US firm with a 'promise of high financial return but no proposals for assistance with management of the wastes or associated training'.[63] In the case of Papua New Guinea, Global Telesis, a California firm, tried in 1988 to get a provincial government to agree to build a $38 million detoxification plant to handle 600000 tons of waste from the US west coast.[64] Fortunately, the deal fell through, though other offers might be on the way.

Military activity has long been a major source of ecological disruption in the Pacific. Indeed, one of the leading environmental crimes of all time was the US nuclear weapons program in the Marshalls, which in 12 years contaminated a total of 14 atolls, most of which were inhabited. According to Marshallese health worker Darlene Keju, 'the list of health problems resulting from [radiation] exposure is virtually endless, and includes many cases of thyroid cancer, leukemia, cataracts, miscarriages, and stillbirths.'[65] Of greater concern to Keju and other medical workers is the increasing incidence of jellyfish-like babies which 'breathe and move up and down, but are not shaped like a human being but rather like a bag of jelly'.[66] These babies live only for a few hours.

The peak period for the eruption of radiation-related cancers is expected 40 years after exposure, which would mean the 1990s. Indeed, all the alterations induced by the tests in the genetic structure of the Marshallese will not be known for some time.

The experience of the Marshalls may soon be repeated in the South Pacific, owing to France's continued testing of nuclear weapons beneath the ocean floor at Moruroa Atoll in Tahiti, in defiance of the inhabitants of the whole region. There are strong fears that radiation may be seeping through the ocean floor and contaminating the food chain. Lending credence to this fear was a rare admission in March 1989 by the commander of military forces in French Polynesia that the testing was being moved to Fangataufa Atoll to prevent cracks from growing in the substructure of Moruroa, where sections of the barrier reef had already collapsed.[67] More recently, Greenpeace researchers have disclosed that plankton samples they collected in the ocean near the testing area contained cesium-134, a substance produced by nuclear testing.[68]

Like Moruroa and Fangataufa, the US-controlled Johnston Atoll is regarded by many peoples in the Pacific as an environmental time bomb. The island houses the Johnston Atoll Chemical Disposal System (JACADS), where the US military plans to destroy not only chemical weapons stored on the island and elsewhere in the Pacific but also those shipped over from Germany. Currently, in addition to its own stockpile, the island has 109 mustard gas shells shipped from the Solomon Islands and 100000 chemical weapons transported from Germany.[69]

Pacific peoples fear not only the release of toxic chemicals in the process of destroying the munitions, an activity that allows no room for human error, but also the possibility that the atoll could become the disposal point for the huge stocks of chemical weapons on the US mainland.[70] Thus, the official communiqué of the heads of government at the twenty-first Pacific Forum meeting in Port Vila, Vanuatu, stated that they

> felt very strongly that the facility at Johnston Atoll should not become the permanent toxic waste disposal center of the world. They expressed their firm conviction that the facility should be

closed down once the current operations had been completed and called on the United States to ensure that no further chemical weapons or other toxic materials would be stockpiled or destroyed at Johnston Atoll.[71]

'The ground is like our roof. If we do not care for it, it will not shelter us and we will die out.'[72] The truth in this saying of the people of Vanuatu has been underlined by the massive ecological disruption that has accompanied over 200 years of colonial conquest, biological colonization, economic exploitation and military rivalry impelled by forces external to the South Pacific. It also points to the way to arrest the downward descent of the ecosystem: the reassertion of the traditional ecological ethic of Pacific peoples that engendered harmony instead of conflict between community and the environment.

8

Strategic Colonialism in the South Pacific

If the Pacific faces the prospect of being the toxic dump of the world, it is partly because it is the one part of the globe where colonialism is alive and well. The United States and France are the worst offenders, displaying behavior that oscillates between bullying and arrogant paternalism. But the region has had to live as well with Indonesia's *lebensraum* expansionism and Australia's 'Big Brother' foreign policy.

The US: from Trusteeship to Annexation

By the late 1980s Washington had almost completed the process of formally incorporating the former United Nations Trust Territory of the Pacific Islands into the United States either as commonwealths (Northern Marianas) or 'freely associated states' (the Marshall Islands, Federated States of Micronesia, and Palau). This absorption of Micronesia into the US body politic is not unusual, for the peculiarity of the US as a colonial power is that, with the exception of the Philippines, most of the territories that were colonized or occupied by white American settlers were absorbed into the US body politic. Prior to Micronesia, the list included Hawaii, Texas, and the other parts of the American Southwest that were detached from Mexico.

The process of absorbing Micronesia began in the early 1960s, when under pressure to decolonize the territory from newly independent countries entering the United Nations, the US set up the Congress of Micronesia. But contrary to the original United Nations mandate requiring the US to prepare Micronesia for independence, the US intention, as set forth in National Security Memorandum No. 145, was 'the movement of Micronesia into a permanent relationship with the US within our political framework'.[1] The rationale was the 'strategic denial' of Micronesia to other powers which might threaten the United States.

Contrary to US expectations, the Congress of Micronesia was an unwieldy instrument for moving Micronesia to a new status. By encouraging separatist sentiments, the US successfully fragmented the territory into four separate entities. Then, dealing with each 'state' separately, the US entered into a separate agreement with the representatives of the Northern Marianas to set up a 'commonwealth' in 1975, and began negotiations to turn the Federated States of Micronesia, the Marshall Islands, and Palau into 'freely associated states'. Negotiations were completed in 1985, and in 1986 the Federated States of Micronesia and the Marshall Islands formally adopted the 'Compact of Free Association'.

Throughout the period of the Trusteeship, the US, in contravention of Article 6 of the Trusteeship Agreement that required it to 'promote the economic advancement and self-sufficiency of the inhabitants', sought to eliminate independence as a viable alternative by not building its economic foundations. As even the US representative to the UN Trusteeship Council admitted in 1969, 'Economic development is almost nonexistent in the trust territory ... Positive and forward-looking steps to utilize the resources of the islands and the sea surrounding them have yet to be taken.'[2] Instead of encouraging development, the US, following the recommendation of the confidential Solomon Report, regarded the territory as a 'deficit area to be subsidized'.[3] A measure of the dependency that was created is the fact that in the 1960s, when transitional talks began, 65 per cent of all Micronesians who worked for wages worked either for the US-funded Trust government or for US government agencies.[4] This dependency naturally translated into a massive vote for continuing association with the United States when the future of the territories was put to a vote.

The one hitch was Palau, which adopted a constitution which banned the storage and transit of nuclear weapons – a provision that directly contradicted the provisions of the Compact, which gave the Pentagon full authority over defense matters. The Pentagon was especially insistent on absolute control because, as a member of the US Office for Micronesian Status Negotiations put it:

> Should the United States, for whatever reasons, elect in the future to relinquish its forward bases at Okinawa and the Philippines, Palau would be one of the logical replacements. That is why the US must secure military rights in these islands against the day when Tinian, Guam, and Palau may become our fallback arc of defense in the Western Pacific.[5]

To resolve the contradiction between the Palauan constitution and the Compact, the US has forced the people of Palau to go to the polls no less than seven times in one decade to repeal the nuclear-free clause. But for seven times, the polls failed to yield the 75 per cent of votes cast that would override the constitution. In the process, Palauan politics became extremely violent, with one president being assassinated, another committing suicide, and many anti-nuclear activists being threatened and intimidated.

What one observer calls the United States' 'remarkable contempt of democracy'[6] has been repeated in its actions toward other island states.

The US has, for instance, refused to sign the United Nations Convention on the Law of the Sea (UNCLOS), which has already been ratified by 41 states. UNCLOS is vital to the island states because it recognizes an 'Exclusive Economic Zone' (EEZ) of up to 200 nautical miles 'within which the coastal state may exercise sovereign rights with regard to the management of natural resources, living and non-living, in the waters, sea-bed, and subsoil'.[7]

Of particular concern to the island states has been jurisdiction over migratory fish like tuna, over which they have come into conflict with the US when they have seized American fishing boats poaching in their exclusive zones. Though the US continues to refuse legal recognition to their EEZs, it was finally forced to negotiate a 'tuna treaty' with a number of island states in 1986. However, this came only after Kiribati forced the issue a year earlier by signing a fishing agreement with the then Soviet Union, which recognized the 200-mile EEZ. Fearful that this was 'a possible precedent for Soviet agreements with other poor but strategically located states',[8] the US finally came to the negotiating table. While the treaty is an improvement over the former situation, many Pacific observers feel that it is still inequitable since the $12 million a year that the US agreed to turn over to the island states was the equivalent of only 9 per cent of the value of the US tuna catch in the region.[9]

The US has also refused to be a party to the South Pacific Nuclear Free Zone Agreement (SPNFZ), which has been ratified by 11 Pacific countries, as well as by China and the former Soviet Union. The treaty prohibits the testing, manufacture, acquisition and stationing of nuclear weapons in the treaty area. Though the treaty is weak in the sense that it leaves it up to the individual states whether or not to permit the transit of nuclear-armed aircraft through their ports, the United States claimed that signing the treaty 'could undermine its nuclear deterrent capability, disrupt the balance of power in the world, and encourage strategically sensitive areas, such as Western Europe, to create their own nuclear-free zones'.[10]

Table 8.1: Political Status of South Pacific Countries

Country	Sovereign Status	Year of Independence	Present or Ex-colonial Ruler
American Samoa	Unincorporated US Territory		United States
Cook Islands	'Free Association' with New Zealand		New Zealand
Federated States of Micronesia	'Free Association' with US		UN Trust Territory with US as Trustee
Fiji	Independent	1970	Great Britain
French Polynesia	Colony		France
Guam	Unincorporated US Territory		United States
Kiribati	Independent	1979	Great Britain
Marshall Islands	'Free Association' with US		UN Trust Territory with US as Trustee
Nauru	Independent	1968	UN Trust Territory with Australia, Britain and New Zealand as Trustees
New Caledonia	Colony		France
Niue	'Free Association' with New Zealand		New Zealand
Northern Marianas	US Commonwealth		UN Trust Territory with US as Trustee
Palau	'Free Association' with US		UN Trust Territory with US as Trustee
Papua New Guinea	Independent	1975	Australia
Pitcairn Island	Colony		Great Britain
Solomon Islands	Independent	1978	Great Britain
Tokelau	Territory of New Zealand		New Zealand
Tonga	Independent		Informal dependency of Great Britain
Vanuatu	Independent	1980	Condominium of France and Great Britain
Wallis and Futuna	Colony		France
Western Samoa	Independent	1962	New Zealand

Sources: Robert Sutter, *Oceania and the United States: A Primer* (Washington, DC: Congressional Research Service, 1985); Jeremy Carew-Reid, *Environment, Aid, and Regionalism in the South Pacific* (Canberra: National Center for Development Studies, 1989), p. 16

France and Nuclear Imperialism

In preserving its colonial prerogatives in the Pacific, the US has found itself in an unholy alliance with France. Unwilling to ruffle its Cold War alliance with France at the global level, Washington has supported France's policy of testing nuclear weapons in Moruroa and Fangataufa atolls in French Polynesia, despite the unanimous demand in the region to cease the tests. France, in turn, has seen Washington's annexation of Micronesia as lending support to its policy of opposing moves toward independence in New Caledonia, French Polynesia and its other Pacific possessions.

France's continuing colonial policy is anchored in a mixture of strategic, political, psychological and economic motivations.

Since the early 1960s, France has conducted 44 atmospheric nuclear tests and 123 underground explosions in French Polynesia.[11] The French authorities argue that these tests in the South Pacific are central to the maintenance of France's independent nuclear capability, which in turn is central to France's pretense to be a world power. The logic of this policy is to sacrifice the safety and stability of the South Pacific to support a military policy that is relevant mainly to Europe (and, some critics contend, has now lost its relevance even there).

The psychological dimension is also critical. France might be said to be suffering from what Stephen Bates describes as 'its insecurity concerning its status as a medium-sized power'.[12] For more than two centuries it has been forced to play second fiddle in global politics, first to Great Britain, then, after 1945, to the superpowers. Possession of distant colonies allows France not only to maintain bases to sustain a global military presence but to sustain an image of itself as being not just a regional power but also a world power.

Economic considerations are also important. The largest known deposit of nickel in the world is found in New Caledonia, which is also rich in chrome and cobalt. All are strategic minerals.[13] The economic importance of the Pacific colonies to France has now been magnified by the Law of the Sea provision of a 200-mile EEZ. The law has given France a total of 11 million square kilometers of sea, 7 million of which are in the Pacific.[14] The EEZs of the Pacific colonies are said to be rich in strategic minerals which can be mined as soon as the technological capability for seabed mining becomes available. The importance of this dimension in France's Pacific policy was underlined by Rear Admiral Gerard de Castelbajac, commander in chief of the French armed forces in the area, when he declared that 'the increasingly important role played by the sea in national economies, the probable creation of economic sea limits of 200 miles, can only encourage us to play an active and constructive role in this sphere.'[15]

These motivations have led France to increase, rather than decrease, its colonial presence in the Pacific.

One dimension of this presence is military. With 5000 troops in French Polynesia and 9500 soldiers and gendarmes in New Caledonia, France had the third largest military contingent in the South Pacific after Australia and New Zealand in 1988. This presence was supplemented by some 2300 personnel connected with the nuclear testing program.[16]

But perhaps the most visible sign of a colonial revitalization has been the increased flow of French settlers to both French Polynesia and New Caledonia. From 52 per cent of the total population in 1951, the proportion of indigenous *Kanaks* in New Caledonia has declined to 44.8 per cent, with people of French or other European origin now making up 33.6 per cent, and settlers from Asia and other Pacific islands coming to 21.6 per cent.[17] This policy of keeping the colony by swamping it with white settlers was laid out in a 1972 letter from Prime Minister Pierre Mesmer to his colonial minister:

> New Caledonia ... is perhaps the last non-independent tropical territory in the world where a country can get its subjects to migrate. Thus it is necessary to seize this last chance to create another French-speaking country. Apart from a world war, the French presence in New Caledonia can only be threatened by nationalist claims made by indigenous people, supported by allies from other Pacific countries.[18]

Indigenous nationalist claims, the memorandum concluded, 'will only be avoided if the communities from outside the Pacific form the majority ...'[19]

In Tahiti, more than 1000 civilian French people have arrived annually, a great number of them to settle on the island permanently. Today, the 30000 Europeans totally dominate the economy, while most of the 70000 Tahitians have been increasingly marginalized from land and the most productive jobs.[20]

With such official encouragement, it is not suprising that French settlers in New Caledonia have intransigently opposed the movement for independence of the Kanak-dominated FLNKS (*Front de libération kanak et socialiste*).

Violence at the hands of both settlers and security forces claimed the lives of numerous pro-independence people including leaders like Pierre Declerq and Eloi Machoro, and contributed to severe polarization during the 1980s. But France, in defiance of most of the countries in the region, continues to reject the FLNKS-led movement for immediate independence.

The Mantignon Accords, negotiated by the key parties in the conflict in 1988, have temporarily lowered the temperature in the colony. The Accords promise a referendum for independence in 1998, with only those who can show continuous residence in New Caledonia for the previous 10 years being eligible to vote. The FLNKS entered the Accords with the hope that their exclusionary electoral rule would allow the Kanaks to achieve a majority vote for independence by 1998. However, many analysts feel that even if one were to take into account the projected demographic increase on the part of the Kanaks, the latter would still not have the numbers to assure an electoral majority for the independence option against the anti-independence alliance of French settlers and the non-Kanak, non-European population, which has largely sided with the French.[21] The prospects for renewed polarization and violence are thus quite high.

In French Polynesia, where France does not yet face a strong independence movement, it has acted more arbitrarily, with Prime Minister Michel Rocard telling the territorial government that it had no power to end testing and ruling out a referendum on the issue in the territory 'because French defense policy was decided by the French Republic as a whole, not by regions, departments, or towns'.[22]

Identifying the nuclear program with the interests of the French Republic has, in fact, led the French authorities not only to sponsor pro-colonial and anti-democratic policies, but even to engage in state terrorist acts, like the 1985 bombing and sinking of the Greenpeace ship *Rainbow Warrior*.

In an effort to break out of the isolation imposed by its own policies, France has recently made a number of controversial diplomatic initiatives. It has tried to create fissures in the South Pacific Forum, which brings together nearly all the countries in the region, by encouraging the formation of a 'Polynesian Community' to counter the Melanesian bloc, which has been very critical of French policies. Moreover, France has taken advantage of the strains among South Pacific countries by fostering closer ties with the strongly military-influenced Fijian government, which has come under severe regional and international criticism for its origin in a 1987 *coup d'état* and for its discriminatory policies against Indo-Fijians. France is now Fiji's biggest foreign aid donor, and Fiji has become tepid in its support of indigenous peoples' struggles in New Caledonia and French Polynesia.

In sum, by persisting in its aggressive policy of nuclear colonialism, under both conservative and socialist administrations, France's presence is not only unwelcome but dangerous and exceedingly destabilizing to the whole South Pacific.

Indonesia and the Politics of *Lebensraum*

In their colonial posture, the US and France, which boast of being democracies, have also found themselves on the same side as Indonesia, one of the world's most repressive governments.

When Indonesia invaded East Timor in 1975, the latter had virtually achieved its independence from Portugal, where a left-led military coup had demolished Lisbon's will to hold on to its colonies. Over the next 16 years, over 200000 Timorese died from Indonesian bombardments, in clashes with Indonesian troops, from famine and disease, and from execution after surrender.

Counterinsurgency has become a permanent feature of the occupation, with entire districts being relocated and forcibly settled in camps under military surveillance. Food production has been disrupted or halted to suit the military's counterinsurgency strategy. Women, in particular, have suffered enormously, according to leading resistance figure Xanana Gusmao:

> Timorese women feel even more oppressed than men. There are so many cases of disrespect to women – violations, abuses, threats. Many women gave their lives for their honor, others [were] subjugated by force. An entire platoon raping a woman, sexually abusing her until she's almost dead.[23]

In the last few years, Indonesia's attempts to improve its international image by constructing schools and clinics have failed to dispell the impact of the heavy hand of repression. Thus an Indonesian study published in March 1990 found the people to be 'traumatized' and suffering from an 'overdose of the military', while Steven Erlanger of the *New York Times* described East Timor as 'one of the world's sadder places'.[24] Timorese have, in fact, seen the recent influx of tens of thousands of Indonesian settlers as marking another stage of Jakarta's annexationist vision, where settler colonialism and economic exploitation follows military pacification. They see East Timor as eventually suffering the same fate as Sumatra and Sulawesi, where millions of Indonesians were resettled to ease the population pressure in overcrowded Java.

The reality of Indonesia's brutal occupation of what the United Nations continues to regard as a territory under the administering authority of Portugal was underlined by the massacre of about 115 unarmed Timorese mourners in Dili's Santa Cruz cemetery in November 1991. The action provoked the Netherlands, Canada and Denmark to suspend their aid to Jakarta.

However, two of the key players in the region, the United States and Australia, have been hesitant to challenge the government of President Suharto on the latest incident. This is not unexpected, as both countries have quietly abetted the Indonesian occupation. Twelve hours before the annexation occurred in December 1975, Secretary of State Henry Kissinger told reporters that 'the US understands Indonesia's position on the question of East Timor.'[25] Uncritical support for the military government of Indonesia, which is seen as an extremely strategic country, has been, in fact, a consistent element in US foreign policy ever since the CIA-backed ouster of Sukarno in 1965.

As for Australia, it has consistently put good relations with Indonesia above the question of human rights and self-determination. This policy is motivated partly by economics. Australia did not want East Timor to get in the way of the two countries' common desire to develop oil fields in the Timor Sea, for which they signed a treaty in 1990. More important, Australia does not want Indonesia, a powerful member of the Association of Southeast Asian Nations (ASEAN), to block its efforts to develop closer trade and investment ties with Southeast Asia. This policy of sacrificing a small state on the chessboard of big power politics was expressed in this fashion by Australian foreign minister Gareth Evans:

> Well, we don't accept that there's any international legal obligation not to recognize acquisitions of this kind ... What I can say is simply that the world is a pretty unfair place, that it's littered over the course of decades and the centuries with examples of acquisitions by force which have proved to be, for whatever reason, irreversible.[26]

East Timor is not the only manifestation of Indonesian expansionism. In the last few years, Indonesian troops have regularly crossed the border from their province of Irian Jaya into Papua New Guinea, supposedly in pursuit of Irianese rebels. There have also been 'accusations of Indonesian interference in domestic politics through financial donations to PNG [Papua New Guinean] political figures'.[27] Not surprisingly, close to 80 per cent of Papua New Guineans, according to one survey, see Indonesia as having a negative effect on their security.[28]

Australia as 'Big Brother'

While the US, France and Indonesia have engaged in old-fashioned colonialism, Australia, the dominant power in the South Pacific, has put into effect what many regard as a more sophisticated neo-colonial approach toward the region.

Most of the island economies are greatly dependent on their huge southern neighbor. Australia is the biggest investor in the region, its stock of investment reaching A$1.6 billion in 1987. Of this amount, A$1.3 billion was invested in Papua New Guinea, much of it in mining operations. Their level of investment has given Australian corporations what an Australian parliamentary report describes as an 'enormous influence on the economies of the Pacific'.[29] That influence has often been exercised in a negative fashion, according to the Australian Council of Churches.

> [Australian companies] encourage consumerism to make a growing market for their products and thereby influence the indigenous lifestyle, often making the local population dependent on them. They compete against local traders to the latter's detriment, and further impoverish the local economy by repatriating their profits. In view of the pervasive nature of Australian Transnational Corporations, Fiji has been described as 'a developing Australian colony' and Papua New Guinea 'an Australian neo-colony'.[30]

Trade between Australia and the South Pacific is extremely unbalanced, with Australia exporting five times more to the region than it imports. The structure of the trade is colonial, with a great part of Australia's exports being manufactures and processed foodstuffs and its imports being largely minerals like phosphate and gold.[31]

Australia is the major aid donor to the region, providing some A$1 billion annually, of which one-third goes to Papua New Guinea. While the government often points to the aid program as a sign of its commitment to the region, some critics point out that 'because of the strong trade imbalance in Australia's favor, aid given to the region has merely in part offset some of the inequalities in the relationship.'[32] Other critics question the very rationale of aid, saying that it has fostered a political economy of dependency as well as served as the conduit for inappropriate technologies. As one analyst points out, the South Pacific countries are experiencing environmental problems stemming from the processes of development and underdevelopment. The two are linked in a growth spiral as the pace and quantity of aid entering the region increases and leads to hastily conceived and poorly planned development.[33]

President Ierema Tabai of Kiribati, which receives about A$3 million a year from Australia, has complained about another cost of the high levels of aid per capita that is flowing into the region: '[I]t is simply impossible to behave as an independent country if somebody else is paying the bill.'[34]

In terms of its strategic political relationship to the region, Australia has acted largely as a proxy of the United States. As an Australian parliamentary committee noted, '[The United States] has focused more on the Northern Pacific area, and has devoted little attention to the South Pacific region, leaving Australia to pursue Western interests on its behalf.'[35] The institutional embodiment of this division of labor was the multilateral defense treaty ANZUS, which, until its demise in the mid-1980s, bound Australia, New Zealand and the United States in the common goal of repelling 'communist aggression' in the South Pacific.

While Australia has refused to follow the US in the latter's support for French nuclear testing in the region, it has, for the most part, served as a faithful supporter of US strategic policies. Unlike in New Zealand, the Australian authorities are proud of their contribution to US nuclear strategy in the form of critical intelligence and communications bases. As Foreign Minister Gareth Evans put it, 'we make a distinctive contribution to the United States' defense posture, and through that to global stability, by operating with the United States a number of Joint Facilities in Australia, most importantly at Pine Gap and Nurrungar.'[36]

Moreover, it was the Australian government that was able to prevent the adoption of more restrictive provisions for the South Pacific Nuclear Free Zone Treaty which would have limited the freedom of US nuclear-armed warships to operate in the area. As analyst Michael Hammel-Green points out, the government of Prime Minister Bob Hawke managed to steer the other South Pacific countries toward setting up a zone that did not bar existing forms of US and Australian nuclear involvement in the South Pacific region, such as nuclear weapons transit, control over nuclear weapons, communications and intelligence bases essential to nuclear conflict, the right to launch nuclear weapons from territorial waters or high seas, missile testing, and uranium export.[37]

Also, the Australian government 'dutifully beat the anti-communist drum when Kiribati negotiated a fishing deal with the Soviet Union [and] ... whipped up anti-Libya hysteria in the Pacific during the brief period that Colonel Gadaffi was a major focus of the Reagan administration's hostility'.[38]

With the winding down of the Cold War, the Australian government has talked less about its part in a global containment strategy and more about a defense strategy oriented toward protecting Australia's 'regional interests'. Under Defense Minister Kim Beazley, the Labor government adopted a posture of 'forward defense' much like the strategy of force projection 1000 miles from its shores that Japan adopted in the early 1980s. Beazley articulated a 1000-mile zone of 'direct military interest' in which Australia claims a right to 'prevail' in a military contingency. That zone covers not only key South Pacific countries but, as critics point out, large areas of Indonesia.[39]

To support its strategy of forward defense, Australia has entered into bilateral defense arrangements with various island governments. The most important vehicle of Australian influence in security issues is the Defense Cooperation Program (DCP), which includes training and equipping of the islands' security forces, regular consultations, reciprocal visits by security personnel, increased deployments of Royal Australian Air Force maritime patrol craft, and increased visits by the Royal Australian Navy.[40]

In recent times, the most important project of the DCP has been the 'Pacific Patrol Boat Project', which involves the purchase of Australian-built and -designed boats by the island governments to police their maritime fishing zones. The patrol boat project has elicited criticism, with some critics claiming that the island governments have been 'coerced' into buying the boats,[41] and others saying that the project may be 'locking poorer nations in the region into expensive and sophisticated defense systems requiring continued expenditure to maintain and eventually replace'.[42]

In sum, while not behaving in blatant colonial fashion like France and the United States, Australia has fostered economic dependency and subordinated the interests of the Pacific island states to its own interests and to the interests of its strategic alliance with the United States. While being more sophisticated in the pursuit of its aims, Australia's foreign policy is still far from reaching the 'partnership' that it claims to be developing with the island states. Not surprisingly, many of the island governments accuse Australia of epitomizing the 'Big Brother syndrome'.

New Zealand: the Consequences of Defection

While Australia served as the United States' loyal ally throughout the 1980s, New Zealand constituted the US' main problem in the South Pacific. When the Labor government under David Lange adopted its policy of banning nuclear-armed and nuclear-powered ships from its ports, all hell broke loose within the formerly secure US–New Zealand alliance. The US proceeded to accord New Zealand a treatment it usually reserved for 'uppity' Third World states. As the former chief of New Zealand's armed forces recounted it,

> The United States' defense guarantee to New Zealand was withdrawn. The flow of information, on which the New Zealand intelligence community was heavily dependent, was terminated. Notice was served that while the restriction on port access remained in place the United States armed forces would not participate in any exercises in company with members of the New Zealand armed forces. Restrictions were imposed on the training courses New Zealand servicemen could attend in the United States and in allied nations where attendance required access to American-provided information or equipment. Restrictions were also imposed on the routine entry of New Zealand ships and aircraft to United States military establishments. It later became evident that further restrictions had been placed on contact between senior US officials and New Zealand Government and Defense representatives. Finally, and most significantly, the United States Government advised that it would not take part in future ANZUS Council meetings in company with New Zealand while the port restriction remained in operation. In effect, that placed a stay on New Zealand's active participation in the ANZUS alliance.[43]

Instead of intimidating New Zealanders, US behavior contributed to stiffening their anti-nuclear stance. In a poll taken in June 1989, 84 per cent approved the government's policy of banning nuclear weapons, up from 67 per cent in 1985. When asked whether they preferred to break defense ties with the United States or allow possibly nuclear-armed warships to enter, 52 per cent chose to break defense ties and 40 per cent picked the latter course. In 1985, 47 per cent preferred to have the ships enter and 44 to break defense ties.[44]

New Zealand's defiance of the US elicited much admiration from many of the Pacific island states. To many, it came as a pleasant surprise, since New Zealanders had earlier had the reputation of being the 'Prussians of the South Pacific', people who willingly soldiered first for Britain, then for the United States. New Zealand's 'new look' did not, however, banish the islanders' resentment of the Big Brother syndrome that New Zealand is seen as sharing with Australia. Like Australia, New Zealand is sometimes accused of being pushy in pursuing its interests, being too ready to play 'regional policeman', and being paternalistic in its diplomacy.[45]

Like Australia, New Zealand pursues a strategic policy of 'forward defense' under which it has bilateral security arrangements with a number of Pacific countries including surveillance of their maritime territories by the Royal New Zealand Air Force. Indeed, the same Labor government that enacted the anti-nuclear policy also carried out a major re-equipment program of the New Zealand armed forces, which included purchasing a new frigate fleet for the Navy. 'The focus in this re-equipment', revealed a high New Zealand official, 'has been very much on the region.'[46]

New Zealand has undoubtedly contributed much to weakening superpower dominance in the region. But it still has a long way to go before the South Pacific countries will regard it as forwarding a genuinely Pacific viewpoint as opposed to that of a western outpost in the South Pacific.

Part II
The Japanese Ascendancy

9

Japan's New Regional Economy

Japan's Rise to Economic Supremacy

In the 1980s, Japan emerged as the dominant economic power in the Asia-Pacific region. During that decade and earlier, the area saw an intense, though often muted, struggle for supremacy between US and Japanese capital. It was the export of US capital that constituted the main external stimulus for the first phase of East Asia's export-oriented industrialization from 1965 to 1980, although Japanese capital was also active, focusing primarily on South Korea and Taiwan. However, from the mid-1980s onward, Japanese capital became the main agent of regional economic transformation.

Although the US continues to be an important economic actor, it is the dynamism of the Japanese technoeconomic machine that is reshaping the Asia-Pacific, as is evident from the following brief survey:

- Japan is now the most dynamic investor in the area, accounting for $41.5 billion in direct investments as of 1989, in contrast to the US input of $32 billion. Half of the Japanese total was injected between 1985 and 1989, reflecting the appreciation of the yen and the consequent search for cheap labor by Japan's conglomerates.[1]
- Japan is now the the region's most important trading partner. While the US remains the number one market for most economies in the region, Japan is pushing hard as an import absorber, and should outstrip the US by the year 2000. In 1989, it took in $70.3 billion of the region's exports, compared to the $101.3 billion absorbed by the US. On the other hand, Japan's exports to the region came to $92.4 billion, while the US exported $67.9 billion.[2]
- Japan is now the area's main source of technology, particularly high technology. In 1987, the value of Japan's exports of high tech to the East Asian and Southeast Asian economies was twice that of the United States.[3] The so-called 'tiger' economies' massive multibillion dollar trade deficits with Japan, which have accompanied their trade surpluses with the US, reflect a high degree of dependence on Japanese technology in the form of machinery and high-tech components.

- Japan is the principal source of bilateral aid to the region, providing $4 billion in 1988, or more than twice the US level. The bulk of Japan's grant and loan program is, in fact, targeted at the Asia-Pacific, a situation that the Japanese Foreign Ministry claims 'reflects the close historical relationship between Japan and the rest of Asia, and the fact that interdependence between Japan and the other Asian nations is deeper than interdependence between Japan and developing countries in other parts of the world'.[4] More candidly, K. Matsuura, director general of the Foreign Ministry's Economic Bureau, admonishes, '[W]e shouldn't simply throw money in random directions. Aid must be steered to places where it will bring long-term benefits back to its donor.'[5]

Table 9.1: Cumulative Japanese and US Investment in the Asia-Pacific Region as of 1988 (in millions of $)

	Japan [a]	US
Newly Industrializing Countries	15015	10881
Hong Kong	6167	5028
South Korea	3248	1302
Singapore	3812	3005
Taiwan	1791	1546
China	2036	310
ASEAN	14784	6800
Brunei	31	NA
Indonesia	9807	3006
Malaysia	1834	1363
Philippines	1120	1305
Thailand	1992	1126
Oceania	9315	13884
Australia	8137	13058
Fiji	43	NA[b]
Northern Marianas	198	NA[b]
New Zealand	593	826
Papua New Guinea	208	NA[b]
Western Carolines	42	NA[b]
Vanuatu	64	NA[b]
Other Pacific Islands	30	NA[b]
Total East Asia and Oceania	41153	31875

Notes: [a] For FY 1951–88
       [b] US Dept. of Commerce category 'Other Asia' does not separate investments in 'Other South Asian Countries' and Pacific islands.
Source: Richard Cronin, *Japan's Expanding Role and Influence in the Asia-Pacific Region: Implications for U.S. Interests and Policy*, 90-432 F (Washington, DC: 7 September 1990), p.7

Surveying the scene, a US government study concludes that the debate on whether a regional trading bloc should form in response to moves toward a North American Free Trade Zone initiative or the emergence of a unified European market is 'somewhat immaterial because a de facto trading bloc is already emerging. It is arising out of economic necessity and, barring draconian barriers, will continue to grow regardless of whether or not free trade among the various economies develops. Japan's business executives do not need free trade to operate.'[6]

Table 9.2: 10 Major Recipients of Japanese Official Development Assistance (ODA), 1985–9 (in millions of $)

Country	Amount	% Share of Total ODA
Indonesia	3159.64	12.71
China	2943.84	11.85
Philippines	1995.81	8.03
Thailand	1676.42	6.75
Bangladesh	1416.71	5.70
India	967.34	3.89
Pakistan	851.19	3.43
Myanma (Burma)	829.73	3.34
Sri Lanka	595.73	2.40
Malaysia	401.98	1.62
Total Above	14838.39	59.71
World Total	24851.83	100.00

Source: Japanese Ministry of Foreign Affairs, *Official Development Assistance: 1990 Annual Report* (Tokyo: Association for Promotion of International Cooperation, March 1991), p. 44

Not surprisingly, the new economic order in the Pacific has spawned updated, cosmetic versions of Japan's 'Greater East Asia Co-Prosperity Sphere' idea. Perhaps the most influential reincarnation is the 'flying geese' theory presented by former Japanese foreign minister Saburo Okita. Asian regional development is presented as a 'process of consecutive take-offs with a built-in catch up process'. With Japan as the lead goose,

the nations of the region engineer successive industrial take-offs and are soon moving on their way to higher stages of development. It is akin to a V-formation, and the relationship among the countries in the formation is neither horizontal integration nor vertical integration as they are commonly known. Rather, it is a combination of both. And because the geese that take off later are able to benefit from the forerunners' experiences to shorten the time required to catch up, they gradually transform the formation from a V-formation to eventual horizontal integration.[7]

A less benign reading comes from the US Congressional Research Service, which claims that 'Japan's goal seems to be an integrated East and South-East Asian economy that allows it to take advantage of differing labor costs, consumption patterns, regulations, and locational advantages in manufacturing.'[8] Integration, in short, is taking place, and at a fast pace, but it is integration of a distinctly unequal sort. This becomes evident from a brief survey of the current relationship of the Japanese economy to the key economies of the region.

The Crisis of the NICs

At the beginning of the 1990s, the 'NICs', or 'newly industrializing countries' – Taiwan, South Korea, Singapore and Hong Kong – were touted as being on the verge of achieving the status of being 'developed countries'. Certainly this was the case if one looked at the per capita income figures for these economies, which had been the prime beneficiaries of the first phase of export-oriented industrialization. Average income per capita stood at $11000 in Hong Kong and Singapore, had passed $8000 in Taiwan, and was $5200 in South Korea. These figures translated into a key market, especially for Japan, which by the end of the 1980s was exporting over $50 billion dollars' worth of goods to these four economies – a figure that was nearly equal to Japan's total exports to Western Europe.

But the per capita income figures masked the fact that by the late 1980s, most of these economies were entering into severe crisis. As noted earlier in the present work, income inequality was worsening in South Korea, Taiwan and Singapore; and industrial pollution had run out of control in Taiwan and South Korea. They were also losing their competitive edge as export-processing economies.

The NICs had emerged as economic wonders basically by performing an intermediary role: that of assembling imported components with cheap labor and exporting the finished product to the US market. Increasingly, this process involved putting together Japanese components, using Japanese precision machinery and licensed Japanese technology. By the late 1980s, this 'triangular' trading system was beginning to unravel. On the one hand, the emergence of aggressive protectionism in the NICs' main market, the United States, was reducing that country's role as an absorber of NIC exports. The US' share of Korea's exports fell from 39 per cent in 1987 to 30 per cent in 1990, and its share of Taiwan's exports went from

45 to 32 per cent. The impact of American protectionism was especially harsh on Korea, which saw its trade with the US transformed from a surplus of $9.5 billion in 1987 to a deficit of $335 million in 1991.

On the other hand, the NICs' deficit with Japan has soared, rising in the case of Korea from $5.4 billion in 1988 to $8.8 billion in 1991, and in Taiwan's case from $6 billion to $10 billion. Unlike the situation in the late 1980s, in the 1990s the two countries' deficits with Japan eclipsed their trade surpluses with the United States.

The rising trade deficit with Japan reflects the fact that these economies remain fundamentally dependent on low value-added labor-intensive production, contrary to official and corporate rhetoric about graduating from the 'cheap labor edge' to the 'high tech advantage'. This technological debacle stems not only from the Japanese' well-known reluctance to share the secrets of their advanced technology but also from the failure of Taiwanese and Korean firms to invest in research and development (R&D). Instead of sinking massive amounts of capital in what they regarded as risky ventures, enterprises preferred instead to gamble on quick profits in Taipei and Seoul's overheated real estate and stock markets during the 1980s. In Taiwan, firms spent on average a mere 0.44 per cent of their sales on R&D[9] – far less than the 4 to 6 per cent of sales devoted to R&D by Japanese corporations. Total Korean expenditures on R&D in 1988 came to $3.43 billion – far short of the R&D budget of just one US company, IBM, which invested $5.9 billion during the same period.[10]

It was hardly surprising then that the level of dependence, for components and technology, that Korea and Taiwan had on Japan in the late 1980s was greater than it was during the first phase of export-oriented industrialization in the 1960s and 1970s. For instance, in 1985, for every $100 of Korean output, the imported input came to $30.6, up from $26.2 in 1970.[11] Taiwan's famous 'computer industry' is actually a glorified description of the low-tech, labor-intensive mass cloning of easy-to-copy IBM models. As for Korea, its image of being a high-tech producer is belied by a few sobering realities: the bestselling Excel subcompact car may be Korea's best-known export, but its body styling is Italian in origin, its engine is designed by the Japanese firm Mitsubishi, and its transmission is both designed and manufactured by Mitsubishi. Korean color television sets may be competing toe-to-toe with Japanese products in the US, but Japanese components account for 85 per cent of their value. Korea may be the world's fifth largest exporter of personal computers, but only the computer cabinet is actually made in the country.[12]

Taiwan and Korea's future growth has, in fact, become hostage to Japanese technology. Japan, for instance, now so completely dominates the making of the sophisticated machines that produce microchips that, as one Taiwanese specialist put it, 'If the Japanese refuse to sell the equipment, you're lost.'[13] And, indeed, the Japanese are not shy when it comes to throwing around their technological weight: in 1990, the Japanese government decided to ban the export of 200 ultra-modern technologies to Korea until 1995 – by which time the Japanese firms will have exploited much of the market potential of these technologies.

Dependence on Japan is likely to be accentuated by the integration of some of the more advanced NIC industries or corporations into the worldwide production and marketing plans of the Japanese conglomerates. Hitachi, for instance, has licensed its 1-megabit DRAM (dynamic random access memory chip) technology to the Korean conglomerate Lucky-Goldstar. One of the key motivations behind Hitachi's move was to acquire a partner that could specialize in turning out a product that was no longer the state of the art while it focused on developing a more profitable product at the frontiers of semiconductor technology: the 4-megabit chip. As one analyst saw it,

> While one megabit DRAMs are currently the industry standard, Japanese producers are gearing up to produce chips that can hold four times as much information. Hitachi apparently can guarantee itself a stable source of one megabit DRAMs through Goldstar, while concentrating on the more complicated and expensive four megabit market.[14]

The same strategy of lowering costs or risks by integrating NIC producers into regional or global production plans is leading the Japanese manufacturers to buy equity in established car industries in Taiwan and Korea. Mitsubishi already has a 15 per cent equity stake in Hyundai Motors, and it has integrated the Korean carmaker into its system of international production by having it produce key parts of selected models like the 'Debonair'.[15] Practically all Taiwanese carmakers now have significant Japanese equity, and they have been reoriented into a division of labor which, in the words of one Japanese analyst, 'is not an equal division of labor as seen in the European community countries, but a vertical one within the automobile industry as a whole'.[16] In this 'inter-product division of labor', the Taiwanese firms will specialize in 'low-price compact cars which have fewer parts and a higher percentage of labor in the entire process'.[17] Perhaps unwittingly using historically loaded terms, the writer concludes: 'China-Taiwan aims for coexistence and coprosperity with Japan by producing the items that are not economically suitable for Japan.'[18]

The failure to 'move up the technological ladder' meant that the NICs had to continue to rely on labor-intensive assembly to provide their competitive edge in export markets – a battle they were bound to lose to the 'would-be NICs' of Southeast Asia. As a result of the drying up of rural labor reserves, the rising cost of living and more effective labor organizing, workers' wages in the NICs spiralled upwards in the 1980s. For instance, in 1989, the average cost per hour of a textile operator came to $3.56 in Taiwan, $2.87 in Korea and $2.44 in Hong Kong. In contrast, the figures were $0.68 in Thailand, $0.40 in China and $0.23 in Indonesia.[19]

A brief examination of trends in Japanese imports indicates that labor-intensive manufactured exports from these lower-wage countries may now be inexorably displacing Korean products in Asia's key market. The rate of growth of Korea's exports to Japan fell from 52.6 per cent in 1987 to 10 per cent in 1989 to 7.2 per cent in 1991. In contrast, in 1991, Japan's imports from China rose by 23 per cent, imports from Malaysia by 25 per cent, and imports from Thailand by 27 per cent. The stark implications of these trends were drawn by one analyst: 'Due to structural problems in manufacturing ... Korean products have been driven out of [Japan] gradually by rival exporting nations.'[20]

Not only were NIC products becoming less competitive in foreign markets, but the NICs themselves were becoming less attractive as sites for foreign investors in search of cheap labor. The figures for Japanese capital flows – the force that is transforming the region – are especially revealing. Between March 1990 and March 1991, Japanese direct investment fell by 56 per cent in Singapore, 53 per cent in South Korea, 10 per cent in Taiwan and 6 per cent in Hong Kong. In contrast, it rose 74.3 per cent in Indonesia, 28 per cent in the Philippines and 8 per cent in Malaysia.[21]

What was more disturbing was that NIC capital was imitating the migratory behavior of foreign capital. In 1990, Korean firms invested over $1 billion abroad, 40 per cent of it in the Third World. Meanwhile, foreign investment in Korea came to only $800 million.[22] The outflow of Taiwanese capital was even more frenzied than that of Korean capital. In 1990 alone, over $6 billion was invested abroad by Taiwanese firms, though only $1.17 billion was registered.[23] A favorite target was Southeast Asia, where the average wage stood at one-third to one-half that in Taiwan. In fact, Taiwan has replaced Japan as the top foreign investor in the Philippines, Malaysia, Thailand and Indonesia. Malaysia alone chalked up $2.3 billion dollars' worth of

Taiwanese investments in 1990; and in Indonesia, Taiwan's $1 billion investment topped Japan's $837 million. The upshot of this remarkable surge is that 'thousands of Taiwanese companies that once faced extinction due to rising labor costs at home have now firmly established overseas factories in Asia's low-wage countries.'[24]

While superficially similar in the sense that both were motivated by the search for cheap labor, the capital outflows from Japan and the NICs were taking place in strikingly different contexts. The surge of Japanese investment into cheap-labor areas was occurring after the country had fully developed its different economic and technological sectors and as part of a process of industrial restructuring that deliberately sought to relocate the Japanese conglomerates' labor-intensive production processes abroad. The capital outflow from Korea and Taiwan was a panic reaction to the disappearance of the cheap labor advantage in countries with many still undeveloped economic sectors, with a relatively low level of technological development, and with sizeable sectors of the population still living under the poverty line. A 'hollowing out' of manufacturing was taking place prematurely in the NICs, before they could develop the skill-intensive, high-technology sectors that would absorb the labor force that would eventually be displaced from labor-intensive industries.

The ASEAN Countries and Asia's 'Second Industrialization'

Asia is now undergoing what is commonly regarded as its 'second wave' of industrialization in the post-Second World War period. This phase may be said to be driven almost completely by foreign capital, something which cannot be said of the first wave, in which domestic actors in the NICs, like state and local business, played an equally critical role. Japanese capital has dominated the process of export-oriented industrialization that is now in progress in Thailand, Malaysia and Indonesia. The key event that triggered this phase of Japanese capital export was the Plaza Accord of 1985, which devalued the dollar relative to the yen in an effort to relieve the US balance of trade deficit with Japan. To counter the rise in production costs unleashed by this process, Japanese conglomerates frantically sought sites where they could relocate their labor-intensive production processes. Since production costs in the traditional recipients of such transfers, the NICs, were also soaring as a result of a combination of rising living costs and US-imposed currency appreciation, Southeast Asia became the main destination of the capital outflow.

Thailand, in particular, became the destination of investment that could only be described as torrential: from $48 million in 1985, Japanese direct investment rose to $250 million in 1987, then sky-rocketed to $1.3 billion in 1989. The rise in Japanese investment in Malaysia was only slightly less spectacular, going from $79 million in 1985 to $163 million in 1987 to $673 million in 1989. The massive capital inflow could not but provoke fairly high growth rates, with Thailand growing by an average of 9 per cent between 1986 and 1989, Malaysia by 6.5 per cent and Indonesia by 6 per cent.

Japanese investment in ASEAN (Association of Southeast Asian Nations) is, of course, hardly new. But the latest wave exhibits several novel characteristics, the most significant of which are the following:

- Whereas previously Japanese investment included a large, if not dominant, chunk going to the extraction of tropical resources like timber and palm oil that constitute the ASEAN countries' natural riches, it is now largely focused on setting up manufacturing enterprises.
- While previous manufacturing investment concentrated in low-technology areas such as textiles and garments, the latest wave is marked by the arrival of the newest equipment and technology, creating what Rob Steven describes as 'the most potent weapon of all: the lowest wages in the region combined with the most advanced technologies'.[25]
- Many of the big Japanese enterprises migrating in the latest wave are accompanied by their smaller-size suppliers and contractors, resulting in the re-creation in ASEAN of the same *Keiretsu* clusters or conglomerate alliances back home, often to the detriment of local suppliers.
- The current Japanese investment thrust is regional in perspective, marked by the setting up of complementary enterprises in different countries to achieve economies of specialization. ASEAN, in other words, is being integrated around the needs of Japanese transnationals. In the case of Matsushita, for instance,

  Each country has a definite function for the electronics giant: Malaysia focusses on color TVs and electric irons (half for export), Singapore on semi-conductors (90 per cent for export), the Philippines on dry-cell batteries as well as floppy-disk drives and electrolytic capacitors (the latter mainly for export), while factories in Thailand and Indonesia are predominantly for domestic markets.[26]

Figure 9.1: Southeast Asian Regional Integration Toyota-style: Toyota Corporation's Auto Parts Complementation Scheme among ASEAN Nations

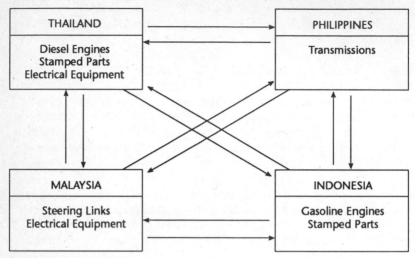

Source: Toyota Motor Corporation

Likewise, car companies like Nissan, Toyota and Mitsubishi have worked out regional specialization schemes. Nissan's factory in Thailand, for instance, produces diesel engines and molds for stamped parts, its subsidiary in Indonesia turns out mechanical parts, and its unit in Malaysia provides clutches and electrical parts.[27] To gain acceptance for their plans, the Japanese firms have appealed to the ASEAN countries' long-time dream of setting up a 'regional car complementation' program. Their investments are not, however, of the sort that would allow the ASEAN countries to develop a truly integrated regional auto industry. The current integration has not been worked out in partnership with governments with a view to maximize technology transfer and other benefits for the participating countries. It is driven, instead, by the efforts of Japanese corporations to cut costs and increase profitability.

The regional corporate thrust has been coordinated with Japan's burgeoning aid program. Japanese aid bureaucrats have unveiled the 'Asian Industries Development Plan' and the 'ASEAN-Japan Development Fund' – initiatives described by one Australian expert on Japanese aid as 'a joint public-private sector activity, which exploits the horizontal division of labor between Japan and Asia, and targets industrial, rather than resources or infrastructure, development'.[28] An American academic denounced the aid program as

Japan's attempt to strengthen 'control over an emerging Asian regional economy' by 'integrating the Asian economies under Japanese leadership'.[29]

The dynamics of the economic growth triggered by the new Japanese investment have brought with them a worsening of income inequalities, uneven development between city and countryside, and a whole slew of environmental problems. Bangkok, where a factory opens every two and a half days and traffic crawls at an average speed of 5 miles per hour, has become a paradigm of the new economic order in Southeast Asia. In the description of the UK's *Financial Times*, 'Bangkok in late 1991 is the economic dream that the industrialized countries and their financial institutions have long wished on the developing world. It is also, in some respects, a nightmare.'[30]

But if one considers the high rate of growth, have these costs been worth it? The trade balance, which is usually a good indicator of the solidity of economic development, suggests a negative response. In 1990, Thailand ran a $5 billion trade deficit with Japan, up from $1 billion in 1985. And after years of being in surplus, Malaysia's trade with Japan lapsed into deficit in 1990. A look at the composition of exports to Japan provides one important clue as to why the deficit with Japan is getting worse: 80 per cent of Malaysia's exports still consist of natural resources such as rubber and petroleum products; 71 per cent of Indonesia's exports are still accounted for by mineral fuels; and the bulk of Thailand's exports is still made up of processed – as opposed to manufactured – commodities. While there is certainly a rise in manufactured exports to Japan, most manufactures are not destined for that market. Instead, Japan is attempting to re-create with ASEAN the same 'triangular relationship' it had with the NICs, in which the ASEAN countries serve as platforms assembling Japanese components with Japanese technology and export the finished products to third countries like the United States.

This relationship, whereby the ASEAN countries exchange raw and processed materials for precision machinery and sophisticated industrial equipment, is bound to lead them into a future of heavy trade deficits, owing to the deteriorating terms of trade against primary products – that is, the strong tendency of the price of manufactured goods to appreciate over time vis-a-vis the price of raw and processed materials. By 1988, 40 per cent of Thailand's total imports consisted of machinery and transport equipment. While much of the expensive industrial equipment coming in was state of the art, there was very little technology that was actually being transferred. Even licensing, the Thai experience reveals, is an inadequate mode of technology transfer, since one is delivered packaged technology, not the learning and application that went into its making, which remains in Japan. Moreover, Thai entrepreneurs, according to the noted economist Suthy Prasartset, are really not interested in genuine technology transfer:

> Their investment behavior is basically to seek a quick return on capital and hence there is a tendency to buy available technology rather than to develop or to combine foreign with local sources of technology. They are quick to invest in activities that yield them the best opportunity for expansion and profit maximization. This means that the corporate sector responds 'efficiently' in promoting import-substituting industries, in partnership with foreign capital, which 'provide luxury consumer goods' to the privileged and relatively small urban population. Such industries are, in fact, imports in disguise which will, in due course, contribute considerably to the balance of trade deficit.[31]

Though they have replaced the NICs as a source of cheap labor, the Thais and Malaysians do not have much time to enjoy their advantage as exporters of cheap, labor-intensive manufactures. While the inflow of capital has been massive, it can also dry up quickly. By 1991, Japanese investment in Indonesia and Thailand was either stagnating or declining. The problem, the Thais discovered, was that there were even cheaper reserves of labor in China and Vietnam. Graduating up the technology ladder is the solution preferred by Thai technocrats, but as in Taiwan and Korea, not only are R&D resources scanty but the technical personnel just aren't there. The ratio of science and technology specialists to the general population is said to be lowest in Thailand among all Asian countries.[32] The total number of Thai scientists engaged in R&D came to only 2700 – compared to 330000 for Japan, 30000 for South Korea (which has a smaller population than Thailand) and roughly the same number in Singapore (which has only 2.5 million people).[33]

In sum, Thailand and Malaysia are being subjected to the same 'structural squeeze' affecting the NICs – a phenomenon marked by the failure to move up to higher-value-added production while being threatened from below by lower-wage producers. The difference is that the length of time it took the ASEAN producers to move from comparative advantage to structural squeeze is much shorter than it was for the NICs.

The Philippines Bypassed

In ASEAN, the Philippines has proven to be a curious exception to the pattern of rapid growth. Although Japanese capital has flowed into the Philippines, its rate of growth has been much lower than that in neighboring countries. The accumulated stock of Japanese investment in the Philippines in the late 1980s came to slightly over $1 billion, whereas it reached almost $10 billion in Indonesia and close to $2 billion each in both Malaysia and Thailand.

Japan's reluctance to invest in the Philippines stems from several factors, including an unwillingness to encroach on what the Japanese have historically recognized as an area of special interest for US firms. But probably more important is the Japanese perception of political instability in the Philippines compared to the other countries in the region, and the relatively low purchasing power of its population. This instability is rooted in the worst situation of poverty and inequality in Southeast Asia: close to 70 per cent of the population live below the poverty line and 80 per cent of the land is concentrated in the hands of 20 per cent of the population. Nowhere else in Asia is the truth that drastic social reform is a prerequisite for development more starkly evident than in the Philippines.

What is unique about the conjuncture of the 1990s, though, is the coincidence of Japanese investors' reluctance and US military and economic disengagement from the Philippines, whose strategic value ended with the conclusion of the Cold War. The Philippines now has greater space to map out a road to independent development, but a vital ingredient is missing: a vigorous and imaginative political leadership that can seize the opportunity to initiate the needed internal reforms that will unleash the economic potential of the country. Instead, the country is burdened with an ineffective political leadership that has restored to the country's elite many of the privileges that were curtailed by the upstart Marcos clique. Deprived of decisive leaders, enduring the lowest rate of growth of a major country in the Asia-Pacific, battered by one natural disaster after another, the Philippines continues to live up to its name as the 'land of missed opportunities'.

China and Vietnam: the 'Last Frontier'

With wages spiralling upwards in the NICs and also rising in the 'near NICs' in the late 1980s, foreign investors in search of sites to relocate their labor-intensive industries increasingly looked to China and

Vietnam, two countries that had abandoned socialism in all but name and were eager to be part of the capitalist mainstream.

The average wage in China was about one-tenth that in Hong Kong and Taiwan, attracting billions of dollars of foreign investment to that country's 'special economic zones'. By 1988, Japanese investment in China had reached $2 billion. Many of the investors were, in fact, refugees from Hong Kong and Taiwan. For instance, Crown Corporation, a Japanese audio equipment maker, shifted most of its manufacturing operations from Taiwan to the Shenzen Economic Zone in Guangdong Province. Another firm, the telecommunications maker Uniden, shut down its operations in Hong Kong and moved across the border to Guangdong.

It was, however, Hong Kong and Taiwanese capital that drew the greatest benefit from China's opening to foreign investment. Guangdong Province adjacent to Hong Kong became the favored relocation site for Hong Kong investors, while Fujian Province across the South China Sea from Taiwan became a prime destination for Taiwanese capital.

In 1990, 63 per cent of the $2.4 billion in foreign investment that poured into Guangdong came from Hong Kong investors. With Hong Kong investors engaged in some 10000 ventures, sourcing their products from some 20000 processing factories, and employing some 2 million workers, Guangdong was in fact effectively an adjunct of Hong Kong's economy. As Hong Kong wages rose, Hong Kong capital did not need to migrate to overseas sites in Southeast Asia to look for cheap labor. And labor in Guangdong was kept cheap by 'the hundreds of thousands of job-seeking migrants who come each spring from other provinces'.[34] These workers turned out products that yielded a 70 per cent profit margin, against 20 per cent in Hong Kong.

Fujian Province, for its part, as of 1991, had received about $1 billion in investment from over 400 Taiwanese companies. The migrant businesses have included electronics assemblers, textile and garment operations, as well a huge chunk – some 225 enterprises – of Taiwan's shoemaking industry.[35] Fujian may, in fact, provide asylum to another kind of capitalist refugee, the Taiwanese firm seeking to escape Taiwan's increasingly effective environmental movement: Formosa Plastics is negotiating actively with Chinese authorities to locate in the province a $7 billion petrochemical plant whose construction in Taiwan has been stalemated by environmentalists.[36]

But the Chinese have not been uniformly positive about the investments of their Hong Kong and Taiwanese kin. Indeed, some of them are beginning to sound like Taiwanese and Hong Kong entrepreneurs talking about the Japanese. Some Guangdong authorities, one report claims, complain 'that most Hong Kong businessmen only cash in on cheap unskilled processing factory labor ... rarely lay down significant long-term industrial investment and look to other countries for high technology'.[37]

Competing with China as the 'last frontier' for foreign investors is Vietnam. For the Japanese, Vietnam 'is a treasure trove of natural resources, with large-scale oil wells and forests, including coal deposits estimated at 20 billion dollars'.[38] But most attractive is the labor force, which is seen as educated, relatively skilled, industrious and, most important, cheap. The average wage in Vietnam is said to be one-third that in Thailand and one-eighth that in Malaysia.[39] The only barrier that stands between Vietnam and a massive Japanese economic invasion is the US embargo, which the Japanese have decided to respect to prevent the already precarious bilateral ties between the two countries from deterioriating any further. The Taiwanese, on the other hand, have not let diplomatic considerations get in the way: as in other parts of Southeast Asia, they have become the biggest foreign investors in Vietnam, pouring in more than $200 million in the last few years.

It is Japanese and western money, however, that the Vietnamese crave most of all, and to get it they have implemented what the International Monetary Fund (IMF) has called a 'model' program of structural adjustment. The key elements of this program are the following:

- essentially privatizing agricultural production by disbanding agricultural cooperatives and giving peasants 15 to 20 year leases on land;
- freeing prices to respond to market forces, devaluing the currency relative to western currencies and moving to end subsidies to state enterprises;
- enacting a foreign investment law that is one of the most liberal in Southeast Asia, providing for 100 per cent foreign ownership in most areas, rights to repatriate profits and a host of tax breaks and incentives.

There is now talk of Japan's making Vietnam its next export platform in Asia, owing to rising wages, low skill levels and massive infrastructural problems in Thailand. The people who are most concerned about this talk are naturally the Thais themselves. But rather than oppose the possible shift, many Thais have adopted a strategy of making Thailand indispensable to the opening of Vietnam. This strategy was laid out by Thai prime minister Anand, who said that Thailand would serve as a 'conduit to transfer Japanese technology, to transfer Japanese expertise, to transfer Japanese experience to these countries'.[40] One Thai official was more ambitious, predicting that 'Indochina will be an extension of our domestic economy.'[41]

Japan and Australia: a Colonial Relationship?

Australia's economic relationship to the Asia-Pacific region has always been ambiguous. While it has filled the role of colonizer with respect to the South Pacific, its relationship to Japan has placed it in almost exactly the opposite position. Japan's role as an engine of the Australian economy began in the 1960s, when, in the description of economist Ross Garnaut, the voracious demand for raw materials in Japan's rapid industrialization was 'promoting new industries and towns across Australia'.[42] In recent years, demand from the other Northeast Asian economies has joined Japan's ever increasing appetite to absorb one-half of Australia's exports of minerals and one-third of its agricultural exports. Northeast Asia has also absorbed the expanding output of Australia's semi-processed raw materials, with Japan alone taking two-thirds of the country's aluminum exports. So dependent is Japan on liquid natural gas from Australia that, as one Australian official put it, 'if the energy supply line from Australia were to be somehow instantly cut, more than half of the lights would go out around the country.'[43]

At the same time, Australia has become a major destination of Japanese investment, with Japanese capital inflow coming to A$2 billion in 1991, compared to A$560 million in 1986–7. While Japanese investment has gone to all sectors, including agriculture and industry, in the late 1980s it focused on real estate and tourism, leading to charges that, as in the US, the Japanese are 'buying up the country'. But as in the United States, the Japanese investment presence has been exaggerated: in the mid-1980s, Japanese investors owned only 3 per cent of total Australian capital stocks, compared to over 15 per cent each for American and British investors. And in real estate, the rapid buildup and relative visibility of Japanese investment has obscured the relatively low level of Japanese land ownership in Australia.[44]

Nonetheless, it is clear that Australia has become much more integrated into the Japanese economy than it is in the economies of the United States and Europe. Moreover, it is integrated into the

Japanese economy in a way that is not far different from Indonesia and Thailand: as an exporter of raw materials, agricultural and semi-processed goods; and as an importer of high-value added machinery and equipment. Not surprisingly, some Australian commentators have characterized Australia's relationship with Japan as a form of 'latter-day economic colonialism'.[45]

What troubles many Australian economic experts is that increasingly Australia is more dependent on Japan as a market than Japan is on it as a source of raw materials, semi-processed and agricultural goods. The Australian Manufacturing Council has called attention to the country's losing its share of Asian markets 'at a worrying rate'.[46] The decline is said to be especially critical in raw material exports. According to one report:

> As a raw material supplier, we may find our standards of living very much at the mercy of powerful buyer-countries such as Japan, whose industries have honed their strategic purchasing skills over centuries. In coking coal, for example, the key Japanese importers work through a single buyer. The importers in Korea, Taiwan, and even Europe find it to their advantage to follow the Japanese lead. New mines in Canada and elsewhere have opened with the assistance of marginal amounts of Japanese capital, adding to competing supplies. Such strategies have been highly successful in pushing down the real prices of Australian exports.[47]

Australian insecurity in the 1980s led the Labor government to follow a two-track strategy of (1) promoting the Australian economy's tighter integration into Northeast Asia; and (2) engaging the United States to remain a military and economic presence in the Pacific.

The justification for the first prong of this strategy was provided in the late 1980s by an important study commissioned by the government entitled *Australia and the Northeast Asian Ascendancy*, authored by Ross Garnaut. Basically providing a conservative, neo-classical perspective to Australia's relations with Northeast Asia, Garnaut proposed three key policies for Australia:

- concentrate on expanding its position as an exporter of raw materials, agricultural goods, processed raw materials and processed food for Northeast Asia;
- press for the dismantling of protectionist barriers to agricultural goods in Northeast Asia while bringing down Australia's own barriers to motor vehicles, textiles, garments and other manufactured imports; and

- work with Japan and other countries to create a 'multifunction polis' located in Australia that would provide 'an integrated work and residential community emphasizing consumerism and incorporating, among other features, "high-tech" R&D industries, leisure facilities, and housing for 100000 people'.[48] Through the multifunction polis, Australia would be able to tap into Japanese technology for the purpose of 'reorienting the wider Australian economy'.[49]

The policy of seeking tighter integration into Northeast Asia is balanced by an effort to persuade the US to maintain an economic and military presence in the region to check Japan and thus give Australia some space for maneuver. As one Australian diplomat put it, 'If the US decides in the end to concentrate on its sphere of influence and leave the area to Japan, Australia would be much the poorer ... It's a lot better for us if we can keep you two wired together in some way.'[50] To keep the US and Japan 'wired together,' Australia became one of the key forces behind the founding of APEC (Asia-Pacific Economic Cooperation), a consultative framework for greater integration of Asia-Pacific economies.

But no sooner was APEC founded in 1989 when its vision of a Pacific community co-led by the US and Japan began to be challenged by a competing vision of the 'East Asia Economic Group' proposed by Malaysia's prime minister Mahathir, which essentially called for an 'Asia for Asians' led by the Japanese. Australia was deeply troubled by the EAEG's thrust for it considered not only the United States but Australia itself as external to the Asia-Pacific community.

The EAEG controversy has highlighted the essential Australian dilemma at the end of the twentieth century: culturally, it was oriented towards Europe; politically, it looked to the US for leadership; economically, it was integrated into Japan's new 'Greater East Asia Co-Prosperity Sphere'.

Conclusion

A process of integration of the Asia-Pacific around the Japanese economic powerhouse was the main feature of the regional economy by the end of the 1980s. This process of functional integration was essentially hierarchical in character rather than reciprocal, with Southeast Asia, Vietnam and China specializing in the provision of cheap labor; Southeast Asia, Australia, the Soviet Union and China serving as a source of raw materials, agricultural commodities and processed raw materials and commodities; and the NICs and Australia functioning as a site for selected less-than-state-of-the-art high-tech industries or projects as well as middle-class mass markets. At the center of this universe lay Japan as the source of capital, credit and technological flows, and the main destination of profits. This process of integration was conflictive, uneven and unstable. The main source of instability was Japan's strong tendency to export significantly more than it imported from most of its client economies, resulting in inexorably rising trade deficits for the latter. This trend was, in turn, a reflection of Japan's monopolization of advanced technology, which allowed it to add significantly more value to its products relative to the low-tech manufactured and processed products, agricultural goods and raw materials it imported from the dependent Asia-Pacific economies.

10

The US–Japan Relationship: from Alliance to Antagonism

The Cold War and the Resurrection of Japan

Japan's emergence as an economic superpower in the postwar period owes itself to many factors, including that country's unique system of conglomerate capitalism with strong direction from the state. However, it cannot be divorced from strategic considerations during the early years of the Cold War. As part of the strategy of containing the then Soviet Union, the US followed the policy proposed by the influential State Department officer George Kennan, of rebuilding the Japanese economy so as to 'permit the economic potential of that country to become again an important force in the Far East, responsive to the interests of peace and stability in the Pacific area ...'[1]

War, specifically the Korean War which lasted from 1950 to 1953, became the mother of prosperity. As a key US diplomat pointed out, 'The US decision during the Korean War to refurbish much of its military equipment in Japan, rather than shipping it back to America, gave the budding Japanese industrial base one of its first shots in the arm.'[2] In 1953 alone, the US pumped $825 million into the Japanese economy for textiles, metal products, fuels and munitions for the war effort. 'War dollars' rose to 60–70 per cent of Japan's exports, enabling key sectors to import technology and raw materials, and embark on rapid economic growth.[3]

After the Korean War, Japan concentrated on the production of civilian commodities, whereas the US chose to devote a great deal of its resources and R&D efforts to military ends. These differing strategic choices had significant consequences, as the Japanese established supremacy in one industry after another in the 1980s.

Three US Reactions

Instead of provoking a unified response, Japan's rise to techno-manufacturing supremacy has triggered considerable disagreement within the American establishment on how to deal with it. One may, however, identify three dominant reactions.

The first is isolationism. Key sectors of US business have practically surrendered the area to Japan, preferring, like the American auto industry, a protectionist strategy of defending the home market or enlarging it via the North American Free Trade Agreement. Isolationism has also crept into the US national security establishment; there are now some people who question the wisdom of maintaining a massive military presence in the area if it will only serve to protect a Japanese economic empire.

In contrast to the corporate world, however, isolationism is likely to remain a very minor current within the national security elite. Isolationism in the US has historically been with respect to Europe, not the Asia-Pacific, which the national security elite has always regarded as an 'American Lake', as a god-given zone of American strategic influence. Though reductions in the strength of the Air Force and the Army might occur, it is unlikely that the Navy will ever allow a significant diminution of its presence in an ocean that provides a great part of its reason for being.[4]

The second response is to preserve the status quo – the US–Japan 'special relationship' – with some minor modifications. Associated principally with the State Department, and to some extent with the Pentagon, this view, which also has been the policy of the White House under Ronald Reagan and George Bush, downplays economic conflicts and emphasizes the strategic alliance. To ease the strain between the two countries, the proponents of this view would have Japan spend more for its defense and increase Japan's share of maintaining US forces in Japan to more than 70 per cent of non-salary costs by 1995.[5] They would also have the Japanese bear the brunt of providing economic assistance for the Third World and use Japanese development aid to achieve US strategic goals in hotspots like the Philippines.

As one may surmise from the Japanese government's subservience to Washington on strategic issues (in contrast to its independence on economic questions), this is also the dominant view in Tokyo, especially within the mainstream of the ruling Liberal Democratic Party and the Foreign Ministry.

The third response is one that sees Japan as strategically an antagonist. There are many in the US Commerce Department, Congress, the Democratic Party and influential think-tanks within Washington who agree with the former French Prime Minister Edith Cresson's virulent denunciation of Japan as 'an adversary who does not respect the rules of the game and whose overwhelming desire is to conquer the world' and the Japanese as 'too busy plotting against the American and European economies to be able to sleep at night'.[6]

Indeed, they would dispute the dominant view among Washington defense analysts and finger Japan, instead of some nebulous 'terrorist' threat from the Third World, as America's main adversary.

They are also apparently attracting some elements within the CIA, which has been an agency in search of a mission ever since the former Soviet Union was dropped from Washington's enemies' list. A recent CIA-funded and sponsored study leaked to the press, 'Japan 2000', echoes Madame Cresson's chauvinist and racist analysis. Composed of prominent scholars, political figures and business people, the 'Japan 2000' panel claims that 'The Japanese firmly believe that "might is right". Their extraordinary economic success causes them to now feel superior to other people. They therefore believe that it is now appropriate for them to exercise dominion ...'[7] Moreover, the 'essential amorality of the *Japanese Paradigm* is in direct conflict with widely and deeply held Western moral imperatives.'[8]

The document, indeed, reads as a declaration of war. Claiming that '"rising sun" is coming – the attack has begun,'[9] it states:

> Our main defense requires us to coalesce a shared vision of our role in the global economy with a shared will to make that vision a reality. We must recognize the power of the Japanese Paradigm and see the threat it poses. We have taken the lead in protecting individual liberty throughout the world. It is now time to confront issues relative to our own ability to survive as a nation and stop the erosion of our position as a principal world economic force.[10]

The Japan-as-the-enemy view is also beginning to win converts within the military, including frontline soldiers like General Henry Stackpole, the commander of Marine forces in Japan, who, as noted earlier, described the US military presence in Asia as the 'cap in the bottle' of Japanese rearmament. As for the Pentagon establishment, as recently as five years ago one could say that the belief in a solid US–Japan alliance was unchallenged there. Several developments since then, however, have pushed it to a more apprehensive outlook.

Perhaps the most decisive was its realization that its advanced weapons systems had become dangerously dependent on Japanese microchips. The vaunted Patriot anti-missile missile, for instance, depends on a variety of Japanese-made semiconductors, including one that only Japan can supply: the gallium arsenide semiconductor. The memory device that allows the cruise missile – another Gulf War star – to remember topography and charts the direction to its target is said to be Japanese-made. The key microchips for the newest type of three-dimensional radar, the phased array, are also reported to be exclusively Japanese-made. All in all, according to a recent Defense Department report, there are 92 types of Japanese-made semiconductors used in all types of US weapons systems.

With studies showing Japan leading in more and more militarily-relevant technologies, the Pentagon has increasingly edged toward the more critical stance of the Commerce Department. Moreover, it has become more receptive to a broader definition of 'national security' that includes shoring up the United Sates' economic and technological strength. And lately, it has become a moving force behind 'industrial policy', an approach that would coordinate government and business efforts to develop US capability in new industries or shore it up in high-tech areas where the US faces marginalization. In 1988, the Pentagon and 14 semiconductor manufacturers launched SEMATECH, a consortium that aims to develop manufacturing technology for the next generation of memory chips.

One of the notable features of the Japan-as-the-enemy movement is that it is strategic elites rather than the corporate elite that are leading the charge: Pentagon technocrats, protectionist bureaucrats at the Commerce Department and the Trade Representative's Office, Congresspeople, and influential industrial policy intellectuals.

This is especially marked in the area of Asia-Pacific trade and investment. The strategic elites do not want to write off the region as a Japanese sphere of economic influence, and they have led the drive to blast open the Japanese market. Except for some semiconductor firms and a few others, on the other hand, American corporations have been reluctant allies, many of them cowed by what it would take to beat the Japanese in their home and regional markets. But the influential role of US strategic elites in Asian commerce is not unusual. After all, as stated earlier, it was the Navy – a strategic elite – that led the American expansion to the western Pacific in the late nineteenth century, invoking the rationale of 'expanding American commerce' to legitimize its strategic thrust into the area.

The appeal to nativism, western culture and racism of the Japan-as-the-enemy school is an explosive combination that will give it momentum, especially as the economic troubles of the US mount. In the hands of skilled populist politicians like the Republican insurgent Pat Buchanan and ex-Ku Klux Klan leader and Nazi David Duke it can become the basis of right-wing efforts to build an artificial sense of national community. Such a development, needless to say, will have a negative fallout on the increasingly apprehensive Asian-American community.

The Japanese Reaction

Not surprisingly, the view of Japan as the threat has provided fertile ground for conservative forces in Japan that favor a foreign and military policy that is more independent of Washington. Shintaro Ishihara (*The Japan That Can Say No*) who favors scrapping the US–Japan Security Treaty and supports Japan's independent rearmament, speaks for an increasingly influential nationalist current of the Liberal Democratic Party (LDP). Also plugging for a more independent path and an expansion of Japan's military might are the Japan Defense Agency (JDA); the powerful armaments industry created by the JDA's 'Buy Japan' policy; and the top brass of the Japan Self-Defense Forces. Reflecting the feelings of the generals is General Hiroomi Kurisu, former chairman of joint chiefs of staff, who wants a bigger military because 'Japan needs the power to protect Japanese interests in [its neighboring] countries.'[11]

There is an increasingly powerful lobby for independent militarization in Japan, though it is curious that not only the LDP mainstream but also the Japanese left downplays its strength as well as the real rifts in the US–Japan alliance, preferring to promote the image of a Japan that is permanently subservient to the US.

One of the disturbing features of Japanese neonationalism is that it feeds on racist feelings that are common even among members of the ruling conservative establishment. A few years ago, one leading official of the ruling party said that one of the reasons the US was lagging was the multiracial character of its population. Such theories can only serve to legitimize racist practices such as fingerprinting and other forms of discrimination that have been directed at Japan's 680000 Korean residents and the growing number of foreign workers.

The Question of Japanese Militarism

The Japanese neonationalists' hopes about Japan's military potential are not exaggerated. It now has the third largest navy in the world.[12] Its defense budget is already the world's third largest, yet it spends only slightly over 1 per cent of its GNP on defense, in contrast to the US figure of 5.8 per cent of GNP. If, following the US State Department's current prescription, Japan were to spend more on its military and devoted, say, even just another 1 per cent of Japan's 2 trillion (2 million million) dollar GNP to defense spending, the result would mean rearmament – and regional destabilization – on a massive scale.

Moreover, Japan's superiority in cutting-edge high technologies like semiconductors, optoelectronics, high performance computing, digital imaging and superconductors can enable it to achieve a breakthrough to high-tech weaponry that would allow it to leap over the nuclear stage. But even without a 'technological leapfrog', says one analyst, Japan would have some rather significant advantages in an era of three-way (US, Russia, Japan) parity:

First of all, the Japanese might be able to use their advantage in production technology to produce weapons more quickly and cheaply than their rivals. They might be able to use flexible production systems to bring the low-cost advantages of mass production to the specialized production of advanced military systems. Furthermore, Japan's reliability advantage could prove to haunt both its economic competitors and its military enemies. While US weapons systems incorporating all the latest electronic equipment continued to malfunction, the Japanese might achieve decisive superiority with slightly less sophisticated but more reliable systems. If Japan could produce the 100 per cent reliable system, would the United States and the Soviet Union be able to keep up?[13]

The antagonistic posture, while still a minority current, is likely to become the dominant feature of the relationship the more the US pushes Japan around to achieve its strategic priorities, as in the Gulf, and the worse the economic relations between the two countries become. Survey findings that most Americans now rate Japan as the most serious threat to the wellbeing of the US are matched by poll results that show that more Japanese teenagers see the US rather than the old Soviet Union as their more likely enemy in war.[14] It is rather revealing that one of the most popular comic strips in Japan today is the saga of a Japanese nuclear submarine that defies the US Pacific Naval Command and declares a 'war for Japan's true independence'.[15]

In this context, *one cannot assume that the still dominant anti-war sentiments among the Japanese will be permanent, or that they will be strong enough to resist the drive of the independent militarization lobby.*

Balance of Power Politics

The prospect of Japanese rearmament has alarmed peoples throughout East and Southeast Asia. For the most part, the elites throughout the region have tried to deal with it by asking the United States to maintain its military presence in the area. Singapore has gone furthest

Figure 10.1: The Asia-Pacific Region: the View from Tokyo

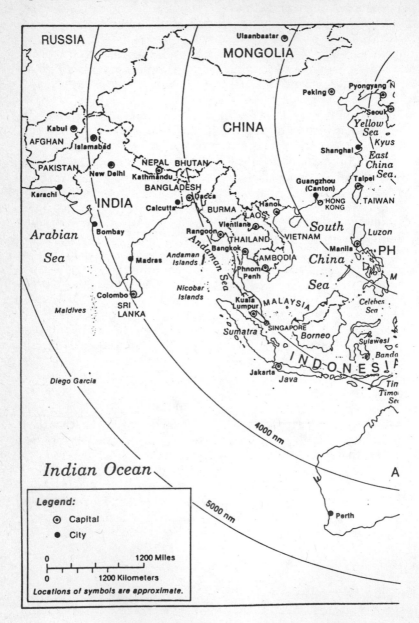

Source: US Congressional Research Service

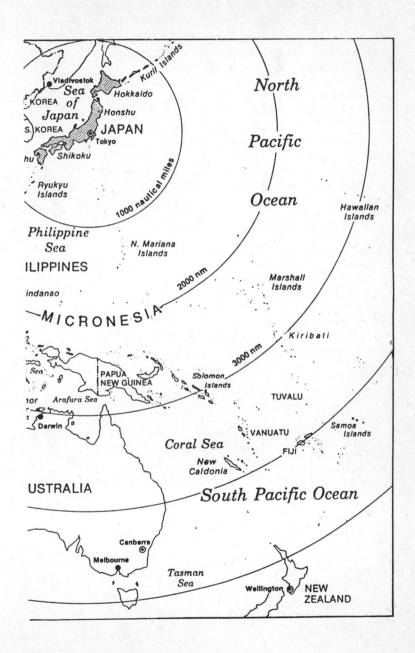

on this path by offering the United States Air Force and Seventh Fleet generous access arrangements to make up for the loss of the US bases in the Philippines. Even Malaysia, while seeking to exclude the US from a regional economic bloc, has not advocated the elimination of the American military presence.

Table 10.1: Japanese High Technology Compared with US and Russian High Technology in Areas of Military Importance

	Japan	US	Russia
COMPUTERS			
Large-scale DRAMs	▲	△	▼
Gallium Arsenide Circuits	▲	△	▼
Josephson junctions	▲	▲	▼
High-speed computers	△*	▲	▼
Artificial intelligence	△*	▲	▼
Charge Coupled Devices (CCD)	▲	△	▼
Infrared sensors	▲*	▲	▼
Acoustic sensors	▲	△	▼
Ultra-sound search devices	▲	△	▼
Millimeter wave radar	▲	△*	▼
High-power lasers	▼	▲	△
Low-power (semiconductor) lasers	▲	△	▼
AEROSPACE			
Control Configured Vehicle (CCV)	▲	△*	▼
Carbon fibers (composites)	▲	△	▼
Titanium composites	▼	△	▲
Liquid crystal displays	▲	△	▼
Jet engines	▼	▲	▲
Liquid hydrogen rockets	▲	△	△
Miniature bearings	▲	△	▼
Extra large machine tools	▼	△	▲
Specialty machine tools	△	▲	△
Numerical control machines	▲	△	▼
Superconductive materials	▲*	▲	△

Notes: ▲ Relatively ahead   ▼ Relatively behind
△ Somewhat above average   * Potential for rapid advance in the future

Source: Steven Vogel, *Japanese High Technology, Politics, and Power* (Berkeley: Berkeley Roundtable on the International Economy, March 1989), p. 33; Vogel's assessments come from *Voice*, September 1987, p. 95

This is, of course, resorting to the old system of seeking security via balance of power politics. Economically dependent on Japan, yet fearing its rising political influence and military power, the East

Asian and Southeast Asian elites see themselves as having few other options. The problem with balance of power strategies, however, is that, as in Europe in 1914 and East Asia in the 1930s, they usually end in the outbreak of hostilities. Trying to contain the Japanese tiger by seeking the protection of the American eagle is precisely the strategy that would make the Asia-Pacific once again an arena of big power confrontation.

Conclusion

In sum, the current US–Japan relationship is not likely to survive the end of the Cold War. The increasingly bitter economic competition is likely to spill over into political and military competition in the next decade, as elite factions that consider the other side as a strategic antagonist gain more and more leverage in both countries. The conflict is likely to have disturbing domestic consequences, with the reemergence to respectability of neonationalist groups in Japan and the spread of populist racist politics in the United States that would directly impact the lives of Asian-Americans.

For the peoples of East Asia, the coming decades pose the threat of drawing the region back into the vortex of global conflict. Increasingly, many feel that the US–Japan relationship is too critical to be left up to the US and Japan to manage by themselves. At the same time, there is widespread worry that the option chosen by many Asian elites – containing Japan by seeking US military protection – is precisely the strategy that would bring confrontation closer.

Part III
A People's Pacific?

11

Towards a New Order in the Pacific

Threats to Peace, Old and New

As the Asia-Pacific enters the twenty-first century, the conversion of the technoeconomic conflict between the US and Japan into a military rivalry is the most threatening development. However, it is not the only potential source of regional conflict. From our survey, we find that other likely causes of regional instability are the following:

- Increased tension in South Korea as public opinion increasingly becomes hostile to the continued presence of 44000 US troops that enforce the continuing division of the peninsula. Despite the recent easing of tensions between South Korea and North Korea, more and more Koreans see the US troops as a relic of the Cold War that must be removed if genuine progress toward unification of the peninsula is to take place. As the US ambassador to South Korea himself recently admitted:

  > The once predominantly favorable attitude of the Korean public toward the United States has been headed downhill ... [The] numbers of Koreans who viewed the US favorably has dropped drastically, from 70 per cent in six years to only 24 per cent today. Even more disturbing to me is another recent poll which found that many students hold views of the US that are simply at variance with the facts – 79 per cent of college students blame the US for the division of Korea, and 64 per cent consider the US to be the country most reluctant to see Korea unified.[1]

- The continuing US compulsion to intervene against nationalist movements that it perceives as communist or 'terrorist'. In East Asia, the main target will continue to be the New People's Army (NPA) and the National Democratic Front (NDF) in the Philippines, but increasingly, the US will worry as well about Muslim fundamentalist movements in Indonesia and Malaysia. The single most worrisome trend in key parts of the Third World for some people in the Bush administration in 1992 was said to be '[t]he march of Islamic fundamentalism'.[2]

115

- Increasing tension between East Asian states and a rearmed Japan. This would be the case even if Japan and the US remained allies. In the last few years, most countries in the region have watched with alarm as Japanese defense spending has gone beyond 1 per cent of GNP (the traditional upper limit), and Japan's military expenditures have become the world's third largest. Asian suspicions have been further raised by the Japanese authorities' efforts to whitewash Second World War crimes in history books, as well as by Japan's growing prowess in militarily relevant industries, like aerospace, aircraft and semiconductors. The US has, of course, taken advantage of these fears to get Asians to tolerate its continuing military presence as an 'insurance policy' against Japanese military expansion.
- The eruption of conflicts over unresolved political problems like the festering crisis in Cambodia; territorial aggression such as the Indonesian occupation of East Timor; territorial disputes such as that over the Spratly Islands on the South China Sea, which involves China, Vietnam, the Philippines, Taiwan and Malaysia; persisting colonialism like French rule over New Caledonia and French Polynesia and US absorption of Micronesia; and complex post-colonial situations such as the passage of Hong Kong to the control of the People's Republic of China in 1997.

  As in the Middle East, conflicts among the lesser military powers of the Asia-Pacific are likely to be fueled by the continuing high levels of military aid and weapons sales to them by the big powers, notably the US, France, Russia and China. Indeed, the weapons trade is probably drawing its greatest profits from the arms race in conventional weapons that has broken out in the region in the aftermath of the Cold War. Also worrying is that in the absence of effective regional agreements, some countries will seek to acquire or develop the capacity to produce nuclear weapons and low-tech weapons of mass destruction like chemical and biological weapons.
- Natural resource conflicts, especially in the South China Sea and the Pacific islands. Conflicts will develop not only over fish and oil, but over other marine resources as well, like tin, tungsten and copper, as seabed mining becomes technologically feasible. Continued US refusal to sign the United Nations Convention on the Law of the Sea (UNCLOS), which provides a legal framework for seabed mining, serves as an encouragement to other big states to flout it, thus adding to the insecurities of the small island states. Similar insecurities are provoked by Japan's continuing refusal to

accede to the island-states' demand for a multilateral fishing agreement like that negotiated with the United States.

- Deepening internal conflicts over the distribution of political and economic power, particularly in the Philippines, Taiwan, South Korea and Thailand; communal conflicts such as that between indigenous Fijians and Indo-Fijians in Fiji; and crises engendered by continued tight authoritarian controls in Burma, China, Indonesia, Singapore and Vietnam. The dynamic of internal and external crises feeding on one another to create situations of regional conflict, as has happened so often in history, cannot be dismissed.

An Alternative Pacific Order

While potential conflicts are numerous, the end of the era of containment is a relatively fluid period that offers unprecedented opportunities to develop a new but lasting framework for regional peace, regional economic cooperation and sustainable development at a national level.

This report concludes by sketching out three proposals addressing critical dimensions of such an effort. These proposals are designed not only to draw popular support regionwide but also win over certain sectors of the regional elites, while neutralizing both Japan and the US, the two most powerful superstates in the coming period.

An Alternative Security Framework

This alternative regional project must first of all address the peace and security issue, for that is potentially the most dangerous dimension of the incipient conflict between Japan and the US, and the specter of Japanese remilitarization is a deeply emotional one throughout the region. This conflict cannot be handled through the balance-of-power strategy adopted by Asian elites for that will only postpone, not contain, confrontation.

An alternative security framework for the Pacific would rest on a simple idea: that the best guarantee of *real security* is the rapid demilitarization and denuclearization of the region. It would build on significant, albeit limited, past successes at a subregional level. The Reagan administration's military buildup in the early and mid-1980s gave impetus to anti-nuclear and anti-military movements throughout the Asia-Pacific region. These movements registered significant, albeit limited, victories, including New Zealand's banning of visits by nuclear-armed and nuclear-powered warships; the virtual disintegration of ANZUS; the creation of the South Pacific Nuclear Free

Figure 11.1: The South Pacific Nuclear Free Zone (SPNFZ)

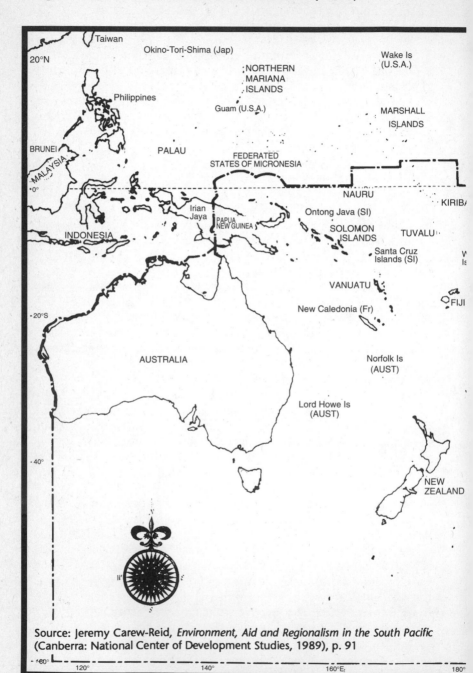

Source: Jeremy Carew-Reid, *Environment, Aid and Regionalism in the South Pacific* (Canberra: National Center of Development Studies, 1989), p. 91

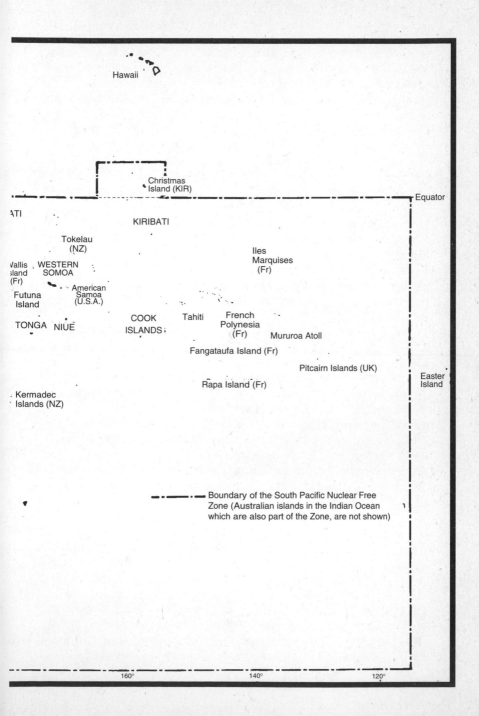

Hawaii

Christmas
Island (KIR)

Equator

ATI

KIRIBATI

Tokelau
(NZ)

Iles
Marquises
(Fr)

Wallis
Island
(Fr)

WESTERN
SOMOA

Futuna
Island

American
Samoa
(U.S.A.)

TONGA NIUE

COOK
ISLANDS

Tahiti

French
Polynesia
(Fr)

Mururoa Atoll

Fangataufa Island (Fr)

Pitcairn Islands (UK)

Easter
Island

Kermadec
Islands (NZ)

Rapa Island (Fr)

—··—··—·— Boundary of the South Pacific Nuclear Free
Zone (Australian islands in the Indian Ocean
which are also part of the Zone, are not shown)

160°   140°   120°

Zone by 11 South Pacific states; the upholding of their nuclear-free constitution by the people of Palau, despite strong US pressure on them to scrap it; the Philippine Senate's decision to terminate the lease to Subic Naval Base; and the North Korean–South Korean agreement to establish a nuclear-free Korean peninsula. While many of these decisions were taken by governments, it is difficult to imagine most of them being taken without strong pressure from popular movements.

Three features of Pacific anti-nuclear movements stand out: first, the solid intertwining of the principles of demilitarization, denuclearization and non-intervention; second, vigorous transborder alliances among Third World peace movements, and between First World movements (Japan, US, Australia, New Zealand) and Third World movements (Philippines, South Korea, Micronesia, South Pacific); and third, successful tactical alliances forged between popular movements and governments (anti-nuclear movements and the governments of Vanuatu and New Zealand). Indeed, so legitimate and popular is the concept of a demilitarized region that some governments have rhetorically espoused it, even without significant popular pressure: the conservative governments of Malaysia and Indonesia, for instance, have urged the Association of Southeast Asian Nations (ASEAN) to become a nuclear-free zone.

The time is ripe to channel subregional energies into the drive to create a regional denuclearized and demilitarized zone that would not only expand subregional initiatives like the SPNFZ but also substantially improve on the latter. That is, the zone would cover more than nuclear weapons and also have tight restraints on the production and movement of all types of weaponry as well as on the size of armies. The principal mechanism to achieve this end would be a multilateral treaty for demilitarization and denuclearization that would involve as signatories the US, Japan, Russia, China and all other Asia-Pacific countries. Implementing this treaty would be a permanent multilateral council in which every country in the region would have a seat and which would be run on the principle of one country, one vote.

This proposal for a multilateral framework for regional security is by no means novel. In October 1990 Australian foreign minister Gareth Evans cautiously proposed moving away from the present Cold War system of bilateral alliances dominated by one hegemonic power, the US, towards 'an all embracing Conference on Security and Cooperation in Asia ... built in some way on the still-evolving Helsinki CSCE model in Europe'.[3] Though the Evans proposal did not propose disbanding the current system of US bilateral alliances, the US reacted negatively to this proposal, as it did to another proposal emanating from Canada to convoke a North Pacific Security Conference.[4] This was, of course, not surprising.

While sharing the multilateral framework of the Evans proposal, the substance of an alternative security framework would be more far-reaching. It would institute, among other things, a ban on nuclear testing in the Pacific; a prohibition on the storage and movement of nuclear arms in the region, by air, land, water, or underwater; a ban on chemical and biological weapons and the immediate shutting down of Johnston Island; withdrawal of all foreign bases from the western Pacific; the pullout of US troops from the Korean peninsula; significant cuts in standing armies, navies and air forces; a ban on research and development of high-tech weaponry; and tight limits on the transfer of conventional arms via sales or aid.

The most pressing issue that must be addressed by an alternative security system is defusing the danger of conflict in the Korean peninsula, which continues to be one of the world's most dangerous flashpoints, despite the recent withdrawal of US nuclear weapons. Denuclearizing the region by pulling out all US troops and ensuring that neither South Korea nor North Korea develops the bomb is but the first step in the process. The root cause of instability is the continuing division of the Korean nation. Thus the alternative security system must also support efforts quickly to reunify the peninsula, as Koreans both south and north of the 38th Parallel desire. Unity of Korea is the key to peace in Northeast Asia, and 44000 US troops stand in the way.

Also a priority issue is ending colonialism and colonial aggression in the Pacific. One way that an alternative security system can address this issue is by calling for a Pan-Pacific Decolonization Conference which would demand genuine independence for Micronesia, New Caledonia and French Polynesia, and call on Indonesia to end its occupation of the state of East Timor.

The fundamental aim of an alternative security framework would be to move regional conflicts from resolution by force and intervention to resolution by diplomacy. Thus, accompanying the sanctions must be diplomatic mechanisms for the resolution not only of superpower disputes but also regional conflicts like the Cambodian civil war and the dangerous multilateral disputes over the Spratly Islands. Such mechanisms would work hand-in-hand rather than supplant United Nations initiatives.

Drawing on their earlier experiences at forging tactical alliances with selected governments at the subregional level, NGOs and progressive movements would need to craft a successful strategy of winning over Asia-Pacific governments and isolating the US, which, being the only true pan-regional military power at this point, would be the state most negatively affected by a denuclearization agreement (though China and Russia might also be recalcitrant). Endorsement of the effort by the Southeast Asian governments, coordinated with a regional mass campaign against Japanese remilitarization and pressure from Japan's peace forces, would contribute to neutralizing opposition from the Japanese government, whose Self Defense Forces still have a major problem with internal and external legitimacy.

An Asia-Pacific Techno-trading Bloc

A second dimension of an alternative regional project is economic: the creation of an Asia-Pacific techno-trading bloc excluding both Japan and the US. While the alternative security framework must be inclusive in order to bind the most threatening powers – and the US in particular – to peaceful solutions, a regional system of preferential economic and technological relations must exclude the two economic superpowers if it is to promote a truly integral development process. That is, while US and Japanese trade and investments would be welcome within the bloc, they would not be extended the same preferential status enjoyed by members of the bloc. This proposal thus parts ways with the 'East Asia Economic Group' concept of Malaysian prime minister Mahathir since the latter would have Japan as the leader of a Pacific bloc.

Preferential trading, investment and technology-sharing arrangements that link the members of the bloc would be the key measures to move the region away from the currently high degree of dependence on both Japan and the US for imports, exports, capital and technology. And in contrast to both the Japanese and US paradigm of corporation-driven regional integration, an Asia-Pacific bloc would strive for a really integral pattern of development – that is, one that ensures that divisions of labor that facilitate trade do not congeal into permanent cleavages; technological know-how is spread around systematically; foreign investment contributes to developing an economy coherently instead of simply creating cheap-labor enclaves; and development proceeds along ecologically sustainable paths rather than the strip-mine pattern characteristic of Japanese and US investment.

One of the key thrusts of the bloc would be to develop complementary interactions between the NICs, especially South Korea, Australia, and the less advanced Asia-Pacific economies, with the emphasis on the sophisticated dispersal of selected low-tech, mid-tech and high-tech production processes and the joint development and deployment of technologies that are environmentally sustainable. Instead of being put at the service of Japanese capital, for instance,

Australia's not insubstantial R&D capability could be harnessed for such a system of preferential sharing to develop sustainable technology.

The destruction of agriculture that is a key feature of industry-focused development within a free trade system would be reversed by the balanced development of industry and agriculture, the encouragement of a regionally diversified agriculture, and the regionwide adoption of organic, biodynamic and labor-intensive production processes.

A common labor code and a common environmental code, which should be popular with the masses, could be made palatable to the more 'enlightened' sectors of the local elites if framed as a 'national interest' issue; that is, regional labor and environmental codes would make it more difficult for Japanese and US corporations to subvert the bargaining power of national governments and pit one country against another by threatening to relocate their operations owing to 'high wages' or 'tough environmental laws'. Indeed, promoting the regional bloc idea as a 'national sovereignty' and 'national security' issue – as a mechanism through which the different participants can both defend their national economies and collectively attain the economic clout to deal with Japan and the US on equal terms – would be a way of neutralizing, if not winning over, significant sections of the national elites.

While constraining the US would be one of the principal objectives of an alternative security framework, constraining Japan would be a key goal of an alternative economic bloc. Free trade ideologues in Washington are likely to oppose the development of an Asia-Pacific regional bloc, but their opposition can be neutralized by sophisticated alliance building directed at US labor and the American environmental movement.

One issue around which an alliance could be constructed is the profound concern of American workers and environmentalists that US and Japanese investors have moved to Southeast Asia mainly to make use of low-cost labor and exploit lax environmental laws to produce cheap products that put more US-based workers out of jobs. The common labor code would eliminate the Asia-Pacific as a haven of cheap labor for US and Japanese firms. And both the labor code and the common environmental code would make trade more equitable by raising the price of exports to reflect the true value of their labor content as well as the cost of protecting the environment. The alliance with US labor, for instance, could be built around the idea of 'saving American jobs by promoting the rights of Asian labor' – which, after all, is really another way of packaging the concept of the international solidarity of labor.

A Regional Congress of NGOs

The third dimension of the regional project would be the coming together, on a regionwide basis, of the non-governmental organizations (NGOs) and popular organizations that form the cutting edge of the alternative Pacific enterprise.

The Asia-Pacific region boasts a tremendous number and rich variety of NGOs and people's organizations. In some areas, these organizations have become as influential as political parties, economic organizations and government bodies. In many countries, the most courageous, dedicated and intelligent organizers are found in NGOs working on human rights, development issues, the environment and minority questions. The creation of an alternative regional order would, in fact, depend greatly on their ability to come together, transcend their specialized or national concerns, and forge a common program.

A regional NGO congress would be necessary to counterbalance three extremely powerful actors: the regional elites, Japan and the US. One of the key objectives of the congress would be to bring regional NGO power to bear on national efforts to promote objectives which the local elites, as well as the foreign actors, are hostile towards: protection of human rights; the spread of democratic government; resource, agrarian and aquarian reforms; protection of the environment; promotion of women's rights; defense of indigenous and minority peoples. Indeed, more effective regional networking between local and national organizations, according to Joe Camilleri, 'may well prove to be the single most important contribution to a more habitable future for the peoples of Asia and the Pacific'.[5]

There is a wealth of examples of successful regional and international NGO cross-border alliances to draw from: for example, the ongoing transregional and transnational campaigns to stop the destruction of rainforests in Thailand, Malaysia and the Philippines; people-to-people exchanges to promote solidarity in Central America in the 1980s; the human rights alliances formed between local human rights groups in the South and Amnesty International chapters in the North.

Another key aim of the congress would be to intervene in the relationship between local governments and the foreign powers. Foreign aid is one of the areas where NGO intervention can make a decisive impact over the next decade. With Japan becoming the world's largest foreign aid donor, the Japanese are now debating the nature, thrust and delivery of aid. There is a growing body of opinion that criticizes both the traditional close relationship between Japanese aid policy and the objectives of Japanese corporations and the American pattern of tying aid to security goals. For instance, an editorial in the *Asahi Evening News*, which is hardly a radical mouthpiece, advocates a new approach to foreign assistance:

It is a task for Japan in the 1990s to provide aid for welfare and growth purposes according to the needs of the receiving countries as well as [to] increase the total amount. It is also necessary to invite the participation of the people in the receiving countries so that its benefits will not be taken up exclusively by a particular group of leaders and bureaucrats.[6]

Organized regionwide, Asia-Pacific NGOs can more effectively intervene in this debate and gain more control over the aid process, which, so far, has been mainly negative in its impact. The result could be arrangements in which the Japanese government is obligated to clear aid projects with local NGO bodies and the regional NGO congress, and the latter's views are made central to the delivery, maintenance and evaluation phases of a project.

An institutionalized NGO watchdog role with Japanese bilateral aid can then be used to lever the more recalcitrant USAID to a similar arrangement. A similar strategy of imposing accountability on the US-dominated World Bank by starting with the Japanese-dominated Asian Development Bank could unfold as a parallel effort. Again, the strategy is to use contradictions to create space for the alternative project.

In conclusion, for the last few centuries, the peoples of the Asia-Pacific region have been largely the passive objects of history, pawns in the chessboard of big-power politics as well as producers of the wealth of others. The last 140 years, in particular, have been a time of great change and trauma, with the carving up of China by the European powers, the opening up of Japan to western trade, anti-colonial struggles, the Second World War and the Cold War. Over the last 40 years, the region has had to live with one central fact, the hegemony of the United States, and with the contradictory legacy of this relationship.

With the end of the Cold War, however, a set of circumstances has emerged which offers the peoples of the region, probably for the first time in two centuries, a real chance to create regional political and economic institutions that would guarantee a future of peace, sovereignty and sustainable development. Will they seize the opportunity? Or will they allow the winds of big power competition to drag them once more into the vortex of conflict and tragedy?

Notes

Chapter 1: The End of the Cold War in the Pacific

1. Quoted in 'The Asian Coprosperity Sphere Again? Options for Japan', *Sankei Shimbun*, 5 December 1991; reproduced in *Foreign Broadcast Information Service, East Asia, Annex*, 9 December 1991, p. 6. This publication shall be referred to hereafter as *FBIS*.
2. Quoted in *Philippine Witness*, No. 38 (September–November 1991), p. 2.

Chapter 3: The Rise of a Pacific Power

1. Quoted in Robert Elegant, *Pacific Destiny: Inside Asia Today* (New York: Crown Publishers, 1990), p. 114.
2. A. Whitney Griswold, *The Far Eastern Policy of the United States* (New Haven, Connecticut: Yale University Press, 1962), p. 34.
3. 'Hawaii Annexation', in Eric Foner and John Garraty (eds), *The Reader's Companion to American History* (Boston: Houghton Mifflin, 1991), p. 493.
4. Quoted in William Manchester, *American Caesar: Douglas MacArthur* (New York: Dell, 1978), pp. 48–9.
5. Roy K. Flint, 'The United States on the Pacific Frontier, 1899–1939', in *The American Military in the Far East: Proceedings of the Ninth Military History Symposium* (Colorado Springs, Colorado: US Air Force Academy, October 1980), pp. 155–6.
6. Griswold, p. 125.
7. John Dower, *War Without Mercy* (New York: Pantheon Books, 1986), p. 41.
8. Quoted in E. Converse, 'United States Plans for a Postwar Overseas Military Base System, 1942–1948', PhD dissertation, Princeton University, New Jersey, 1984, p. 155.
9. 'Conversation Between General of the Army MacArthur and George Kennan, 5 March 1948 – Top Secret', in Thomas Etzold and John Lewis Gaddis (eds), *Containment: Documents on American Policy and Strategy, 1949–50* (New York: Columbia University Press, 1978), p. 229.
10. See the discussion in Franz Schurmann, *The Logic of World Power* (New York: Pantheon Books, 1974), especially pp. 3–46.
11. 'United States Objectives and Programs for National Security' (NSC 68), top secret, 14 April 1950; reproduced in Etzold and Gaddis (eds), p. 441.
12. Gabriel Kolko, *Confronting the Third World* (New York: Pantheon Books, 1988), p. 31.
13. Ibid.

14. Ibid., pp. 32–3.
15. Quoted in Lars Schoultz, *Human Rights and US Policy Toward Latin America* (Princeton, New Jersey: Princeton University Press, 1981), p. 23.
16. Neil Sheehan, *A Bright Shining Lie* (New York: Random House, 1988), p. 155.
17. Quoted in ibid., p. 535.
18. Quoted in Ken Coates, *The Most Dangerous Decade* (London: Spokesman, 1984), p. 135.
19. Ibid.
20. Sheehan, p. 155.
21. Richard Holbrooke, 'US Position in the Pacific', *Current Policy Series*, No. 154, US State Department, Washington, DC, 27 March 1980, p. 1.
22. Paul Nitze *et al.*, *Securing the Seas: The Soviet Naval Challenge and Alliance Options* (Boulder, Colorado: Westview Press, 1977), p. 13.
23. Bernard Trainor, Speech to Naval War College, 21 June 1984, declassified under Freedom of Information Act.
24. Quoted in 'President Disputes General on War Probability', *Washington Post*, 23 June 1984, p. 11.
25. Summarized in *Defense Week*, 14 February 1984, p. 16.

Chapter 4: US Pacific Command Today

1. Most of the following facts and figures are drawn from Walden Bello, Peter Hayes and Lyuba Zarsky, *American Lake: The Nuclear Peril in the Pacific* (London: Penguin, 1987) and Walden Bello, Peter Hayes and Lyuba Zarsky, 'The Bases of Power', unpublished manuscript, 1987.
2. Pacific Campaign to Disarm the Seas, 'The Bush and Gorbachev Nuclear Arms Cuts Proposals', briefing paper, December 1991, p. 6.
3. Admiral George Steele, 'The Seventh Fleet', *Proceedings of the US Naval Institute*, January 1976, p. 30.
4. Carolyn Bowen Francis, 'Base Prostitution in Okinawa', *Japan Militarism Monitor*, No. 49 (May–June 1991), p. 11.
5. Owen Wilkes and Marie Leadbetter, 'The Asia-Pacific Situation', paper presented at Asia-Pacific People's Conference on Peace and Development, Manila, January 1989, p. 6.
6. Mary Lord, Testimony at Hearing of US House of Representatives, Subcommittee on Public Lands and National Parks, Washington, DC, 25 September 1984.
7. Catherine Lutz, Testimony before House of Representatives, Subcommittee on Public Lands and National Parks, Washington, DC, 25 September 1984.
8. See D. Rubinstein, 'Epidemic Disease Among Micronesian Adolescents', in Catherine Lutz (ed.), *Micronesia as Strategic Colony* (Cambridge, Massachusetts: Cultural Survival, 1984), pp. 52–65.
9. Paul Kreisberg, 'Containment's Last Gasp', *Foreign Policy*, No. 75 (Summer 1989), p. 163.
10. Admiral Charles Larson, Statement before US Senate Armed Services Committee, Washington, DC, 13 March 1991, p. 5.

11. Seema Sirohi, 'US Arms Makers' Post-Cold War Scenarios', *Pacific News Service*, 15–19 April 1991.
12. *Washington Post*, 27 March 1990.

Chapter 5: Missionary Democracy and US Foreign Policy

1. The following analysis of the Philippine experience is drawn from Walden Bello and John Gershman, 'Democratization and Stabilization in the Philippines', *Critical Sociology*, Vol. 7, No. 1 (Spring 1990), pp. 35–56.
2. Neil Sheehan, *A Bright Shining Lie* (New York: Random House, 1988), p. 131.
3. Frances Fitzgerald, *Fire in the Lake* (New York: Random House, 1973), p. 116.
4. See, among others, William Blum, *The CIA: A Forgotten History* (London: Zed Books, 1986), pp. 108–12.
5. See Samuel Huntingdon, *Political Order in Changing Societies* (New Haven, Connecticut: Yale University Press, 1968).
6. Quoted in Thomas Powers, *The Man Who Kept the Secrets* (New York: Pocket Books, 1979), p. 250.
7. US Senate Foreign Relations Committee Staff, *Korea and the Philippines* (Washington, DC: US Government Printing Office, 1973).
8. Jeane Kirkpatrick, 'Dictatorships and Double Standards', *Commentary*, July 1979, p. 37.

Chapter 6: The Economic Dimension of Expansionism

1. 'Hawaii Annexation', in Eric Foner and John Garraty (eds), *The Reader's Companion to American History* (Boston: Houghton Mifflin, 1991), p. 493.
2. Much of the following presentation on the Philippine economy during the colonial period (1899–1946) is drawn from the following sources: Yoshihara Kunio, *Philippine Industrialization: Foreign and Domestic Capital* (Singapore: Oxford University Press, 1985); Frank Golay, '"Manila Americans" and Philippine Society: The Voice of Philippine Business', in Norman Owen (ed.), *The Philippine Economy and the United States: Studies in Past and Present Interactions* (Ann Arbor, Michigan: Center for South and Southeast Asian Studies, University of Michigan, 1983), pp. 1–35; and Frank Golay, 'Taming the American Multinationals', in ibid., pp. 131–76.
3. A. Whitney Griswold, *The Far Eastern Policy of the United States* (New Haven, Connecticut: Yale University Press, 1962), p. 469.
4. Gabriel Kolko, *Confronting the Third World* (New York: Pantheon Books, 1988), p. 60.
5. Ibid.
6. Robert McNamara, *1975 Address to the Board of Governors* (Washington, DC: World Bank, 1975), pp. 28–9.
7. Berch Beberoglu, cited in Bennett Harrison and Barry Bluestone, *The Great U-Turn* (New York: Basic Books, 1988), p. 27.

8. Robert Lipsey, 'Changing Patterns of International Investment in and by the United States', in Martin Feldstein (ed.), *The United States in the World Economy* (Chicago: University of Chicago Press, 1988), p. 499.

9. Joseph Grunwald and Kenneth Flamm, *The Global Factory: Foreign Assembly in International Trade* (Washington, DC: Brookings Institution, 1985), p. 3.

10. Ibid., p. 19.

11. Ibid.

12. Pat Choate, *Agents of Influence* (New York: Alfred Knopf, 1990), p. 82.

13. Constantine Markides and Norman Berg, 'Manufacturing Abroad is Bad Business', Harvard Business Review, No. 5 (September–October 1988), p. 115.

14. *Business International*, 29 November, 1985. Cited in Lim Chong Yah *et al.*, *Policy Options for the Singapore Economy* (Singapore: McGraw-Hill, 1988), p. 262.

15. Douglas Sease, 'US Firms Fuel Taiwan's Trade Surplus', *Asian Wall Street Journal*, 8 June 1987, p. 1.

16. Choi Jang-Jip, 'Interest Control and Political Control in South Korea: A Study of Labor Unions in Manufacturing Industries, 1961–1980', PhD dissertation, Department of Political Science, University of Chicago, August 1983, p. 339.

17. George Fitting, 'Export Processing Zones in Taiwan and the Republic of China', *Asian Survey*, Vol. 22, No. 8 (August 1982), p. 737.

18. Rebecca Cantwell *et al.*, *Made in Taiwan: A Human Rights Investigation* (New York: Clergy and Laity Concerned, 1978); quoted in Richard Kagan, 'The "Miracle" of Taiwan', unpublished manuscript, Institute for Food and Development Policy, San Francisco, 1982, p. 67.

19. Quoted in Denis Simon, 'Taiwan, Technology Transfer, and Transnationalism: The Political Management of Dependency', PhD dissertation, University of California, Berkeley, 1980, p. 389.

20. Lee Jeong-Taik, 'Dynamics of Labor Control and Labor Protest in the Process of Export-Oriented Industrialization in South Korea', *Asian Perspective* (Korea), Vol. 12, No. 1 (Spring–Summer 1988), p. 145.

21. Ibid., p. 146.

22. Kagan, p. 68.

23. Hans Luther, 'The Repression of Labour Protest in Singapore: Unique Case or Future Model', *Development and Change*, No. 10 (1979), p. 297.

24. Choi Jang-Jip, pp. 139–40.

25. Ibid., pp. 270–1.

26. KPMG, *The Asia-Pacific Region: Economic and Business Prospects* (Amsterdam, 1988), p. 4.

27. Economic Planning Board, cited in Choi Young-Il, 'Distribution of Wealth: A Critical Issue in South Korea, *Korea Report* (Washington, DC), September–October 1987, p. 8.

28. Simon Long, *Taiwan to 1993: Politics Versus Prosperity*, Special Report No. 1159 (London: Economist Intelligence Unit, 1989), p. 54.

29. Catholic Institute for International Relations (CIIR), *Disposable People: Forced Evictions in South Korea* (London: Catholic Institute for International Relations, 1988), p. 9.
30. Fan Liang-Shing, 'Taiwan's International Reserve Accumulation: Causes and Effects', paper delivered at Conference on Taiwan Economy and Trade, Washington, DC, 18–20 April 1990, p. 14; Lincoln Kaye, 'Sleep-In for Housing', *Far Eastern Economic Review*, 7 September 1989, p. 42.
31. Suthy Prasartset, *Democratic Alternatives to Maldevelopment: The Case of Thailand* (Yokohama: International Peace Research Institute Meigaku [Prime], 1991), p. 9.
32. Larry Burmeister, *Research, Realpolitik, and Development in Korea: The State and the Green Revolution* (Boulder, Colarado: Westview Press, 1988), p. 68.
33. Quoted in Kagan, p. 37.
34. 'As Farm Debt Rises, Farm Population Plummets', *Sindong-A*, April 1989; reproduced in *FBIS: East Asia*, 9 August 1989, p. 40.
35. 'Sympathy for South Korea', *Financial Times*, 22 March 1990.
36. Personal interview with Lee So-Sun by Walden Bello, Seoul, 20 May 1988.

Chapter 7: Ecological Disequilibrium

1.   'Study Shows Third of Sumatra's Forests Have Disappeared Since 1982', *Agence France Press (AFP)*, 11 September 1991; reproduced in *FBIS: Environmental Issues*, 15 November 1991, p. 24.
2.   International Burma Campaign, *Burma Today: Land of Hope and Terror* (Washington, DC: International Burma Campaign, 1991), p. 23.
3.   John Hamilton and Pratap Chatterjee, 'Developing Disaster: The World Bank and Deforestation in Thailand', *Food First Action Alert*, Summer 1991.
4.   'Agriculture Ministry Warns Against Forest Depletion', *SPK* (Kampuchea Radio), 26 May 1991; reproduced in *FBIS: Environmental Issues*, 17 June 1991, p. 12.
5.   'Forest Conservation Policy Outlined', *Dao Siam*, 26 May 1991; reproduced in *FBIS: Environmental Issues*, 13 September 1991, p. 23.
6.   World Rainforest Movement, *Rainforest Destruction: Causes, Effects, and Solutions* (Penang: World Rainforest Movement, 1990), p. 28.
7.   International Burma Campaign, p. 23.
8.   Quoted in *International Solidarity News Digest*, No. 67 (December 1991), p. 2.
9.   Suthy Prasartset, *Democratic Alternatives to Maldevelopment: The Case of Thailand* (Yokohama: International Peace Research Institute Meigaku [Prime], 1991), p. 14.
10. Asian Development Bank, *Economic Policies for Sustainable Development* (Manila: Asian Development Bank, 1990), pp. 45, 49.
11. Richard Tucker, 'The Commercial Timber Economy Under Two Colonial Regimes', in John Dargavel *et al.*, *Changing Tropical Forests: Historical Perspectives on Today's Challenges in Asia, Australasia, and Oceania* (Canberra: Center for Research and Environmental Studies, Australian National University, 1988), p. 223.

12. Ibid., pp. 222–8.
13. Quoted in ibid.
14. Ibid.
15. *International Solidarity News Digest*, No. 67 (December 1991), p. 2.
16. Graham Hancock, *Lords of Poverty* (New York: Atlantic Monthly Press, 1989), pp. 134–8.
17. Hamilton and Chatterjee, pp. 2–3.
18. Quoted in David Lamb, 'A Radical Approach to Tropical Forestry: An Account of Pulpwood Logging in Papua New Guinea', in John Dargavel *et al.*, p. 414.
19. Ibid., p. 415.
20. 'Environmental Damage by Joint Japanese Firm to be Investigated', *Radio Australia*, 15 May 1991; reproduced in *FBIS: Environmental Issues*, 17 June 1991, p. 14.
21. Ibid., pp. 14–15.
22. See account in Walden Bello *et al.*, *Development Debacle: The World Bank in the Philippines* (San Francisco: Institute for Food and Development Policy, 1982), pp. 56–7.
23. Bruce Rich, 'The Emperor's New Clothes: The World Bank and Environmental Reform', *World Policy Journal*, Vol. VII, No. 2 (Spring 1990), p. 312; also 'Kedung Ombo', *Bankcheck,* September 1990, p. 7.
24. 'On Goes Pak Mun', *World Rivers Review*, Vol. 6, No. 3 (May–June 1991), p. 12.
25. 'Three Gorges', *Bankcheck*, September 1990, p. 6.
26. 'China: Three Gorges Project', Memo to Probe International from Shahid Javed Burki, Director, China Country Department, World Bank, Washington, DC, 17 October 1990, p. 2.
27. Ibid.
28. Mark Valencia, 'International Conflict Over Marine Resources in Southeast Asia: Trends in Politicization and Militarization', in Lim Teck Ghee and Mark J. Valencia (eds), *Conflict over Natural Resources in Southeast Asia and the Pacific* (Singapore: Oxford University Press, 1990), p. 110.
29. Asian Development Bank, p. 49.
30. Ibid.
31. Vandana Shiva, 'Environment in Asia', unpublished study done for UNESCO, February 1989, p. 87.
32. Geoffrey Pomeroy, 'Labor and Environmentalists in the Industrializing Nations', unpublished paper, Medford, Massachusetts, 1 May 1989, p. 30.
33. Shiva, p. 109.
34. Personal interview with Michael Hsiao by Walden Bello, Taipei, 12 May 1988.
35. Wang Sung-Hsing and Raymond Apthorpe, *Rice Farming in Taiwan: Three Case Studies* (Taipei: Academia Sinica, 1974), p. 168.
36. Ibid., pp. 169–70.
37. Personal interview with Michael Hsiao by Walden Bello, Taipei, 12 May 1988.
38. Ibid.

39. Shiva, p. 87.
40. Ibid., pp. 108–9.
41. National Research Council, *Alternative Agriculture* (Washington, DC: National Academy Press, 1989), p. 7.
42. Neal Rudge, 'Edgar Lin', *Bang*, March 1988, p. 12.
43. Helen White, 'Thailand's Environment Feels Increasing Strain as Years of Rapid Economic Growth Exact Toll', *Asian Wall Street Journal*, 27 May 1991, p. 14.
44. 'Polluters Considered Criminals', *Yonhap*, 25 March 1991; reproduced in *FBIS: East Asia*, 26 March 1991, p. 32.
45. 'The Environment: A Survey', *The Economist*, 2 September 1989, p. 7; *Cooperative Energy Assessment* (Argonne, Illinois: Republic of Korea Ministry of Energy and US Department of Energy, September 1981), p. 26.
46. White, p. 14.
47. Noh Yang-Keun, 'The Safety Problems of Nuclear Power Plants', *Korea Times*, 30 October 1988, p. 8; 'Korea Will Need 55 Nuclear Power Plants by Year 2031', *Korea Times*, 1 June 1989.
48. Li Wunan, 'Managing Nuclear Wastes in Taiwan', *NATPA Bulletin*, Vol. 7, No. 1 (February 1988), p. 38.
49. *Japan Economic Journal*, 23 February 1991, p. 14.
50. Jeremy Carew-Reid, *Environment, Aid, and Regionalism* (Canberra: National Center for Development Studies/Research School of Pacific Studies, 1989), p. 143.
51. 'Global Warming Threatens Existence of Tokelau Atolls', *Radio Australia*, 24 September 1991; reproduced in *FBIS: Environmental Issues*, 24 September 1991, p. 27.
52. Carew-Reid, pp. 100–1.
53. Ibid., p. 101.
54. 'New Zealand Group Criticizes Japanese Fishing Methods', *AFP*, 25 March 1991; reproduced in *FBIS: Environmental Issues*, 7 May 1991, p. 19.
55. Carew-Reid, p. 89.
56. Ibid., p. 132.
57. Ibid.
58. Ibid., p. 86.
59. *Environmental Aspects of Transnational Corporation Activities in Pollution-Intensive Industries in Selected Asian and Pacific Countries* (New York: United Nations, 1990), pp. 150–1.
60. Carew-Reid, pp. 142–3.
61. Ibid., p. 87.
62. Ibid.
63. Ibid., p. 142.
64. Ron Chepesiuk, 'From Cash to Ash', *E Magazine*, July–August 1991, p. 32.
65. Darlene Keju-Johnson, 'Marshall Islands, Mon Amour', in *Marshall Islands: 37 Years After: Report of a World Council of Churches Delegation to the Marshall Islands, May 20–June 4, 1983* (Geneva: Commission of the Churches in International Affairs, World Council of Churches, 1983), pp. 31–2.

66. Ibid.
67. Stephen Bates, *The South Pacific Countries and France: A Study in Inter-State Relations* (Canberra: Department of International Relations, Research School of Pacific Studies, Australian National University, 1990), p. 38.
68. 'Greenpeace Warns of Nuclear Pollution in South Pacific', *AFP*, 24 June 1991; reproduced in *FBIS: Environmental Issues,* 9 July 1991, p. 39.
69. 'Johnston Update', *Pacific News Bulletin,* Vol. 6, No. 7 (July 1991), p. 3.
70. 'Johnston Update', *Pacific News Bulletin,* Vol. 5, No. 10 (October 1990), p. 2.
71. 'Communiqué' of 21st South Pacific Forum, Port Vila, Vanuatu, 31 July–1 August 1990; reproduced in Peter Plomka (ed.), *The Security of Oceania in the 1990s*, Vol. 2 (Canberra: Strategic and Defense Studies Center, Research School of Pacific Studies, Australian National University, 1990), p. 84.
72. Cited in Carew-Reid, p. 26.

Chapter 8: Strategic Colonialism in the South Pacific

1. Anthony Solomon *et al.*, 'Report by the US Government Survey Mission to the Trust Territory of the Pacific Islands', Washington, DC, 9 October 1963, p. S–5.
2. Quoted in John Hinck, 'The Republic of Palau and the United States: Self-Determination Becomes the Price of Free Association', *California Law Review*, Vol. 78, No. 4 (July 1990), p. 939.
3. Quoted in footnote no. 171 in ibid., p. 938.
4. Sue Roff, *Overreaching in Paradise: United States Policy in Palau Since 1945* (Juneau, Alaska: Denali Press, 1991), p. 61.
5. Richard Teare, interview in film *Strategic Trust: The Making of Nuclear-Free Palau.*
6. David Robie, *Blood on Their Banner: Nationalist Struggles in the South Pacific* (London: Zed Books, 1989), p. 176.
7. World Commission on Environment and Development, *Our Common Future* (New York: Oxford University Press, 1987).
8. Robert Sutter, *Oceania and the United States: A Primer* (Washington, DC: Congressional Research Service, 1985), p. 26.
9. James Anthony, 'Conflict over Natural Resources in the Pacific', in Lim Teck Ghee and Mark J. Valencia (eds), *Conflict over Natural Resources in Southeast Asia and the Pacific* (Singapore: Oxford University Press, 1990), pp. 220–1.
10. Ibid., p. 196.
11. Marie-Therese Danielsson, 'Women's Voices in the Pacific', *Pacific Vision*, Vol. 4, Nos 3 and 4 (November 1991), p. 34.
12. Stephen Bates, *The South Pacific Island Countries and France* (Canberra: Department of International Relations, Research School of Pacific Studies, Australian National University, 1990), p. 20.
13. Ibid., p. 17.
14. Ibid.
15. Ibid., p. 19.

16.   Ibid., pp. 5–6.
17.   *From New Caledonia to Kanaky: Report on a Visit by Australian NGOs* (Canberra: Australian Council for Overseas Aid, 1990), p. 5.
18.   Helen Fraser, *New Caledonia: Anti-Colonialism in a Pacific Territory* (Canberra: Peace Research Center, Research School of Pacific Studies, Australian National University, 1988), p. 6.
19.   Ibid.
20.   Danielsson, p. 33.
21.   See Bates, p. 130; also Charles Pidjot, 'New Caledonia: From Enfant Terrible to Oceanic Partner', in David Hegarty and Peter Polomka (eds), *The Security of Oceania in the 1990s*, Vol. 1 (Canberra: Strategic and Defense Studies Center, Research School of Pacific Studies, 1989), p. 55.
22.   Bates, p. 128.
23.   Quoted in *East Timor: Keeping the Flame of Freedom Alive* (Canberra: Australian Council for Overseas Aid, 1991), p. 20.
24.   Quoted in ibid., p. 4.
25.   Sasha Stepan, *Credibility Gap: Australia and the Timor Gap Treaty* (Canberra: Australian Council for Overseas Aid, 1990), p. 12.
26.   Quoted in *East Timor*, pp. 26–7.
27.   Joint Committee on Foreign Affairs, Defense, and Trade, Parliament of Australia, *Australia's Relations With the South Pacific* (Canberra: Australian Government Publishing Service, March 1989), p. 207.
28.   Stephen Bates, 'South Pacific Island Perceptions of Security', in Peter Polomka (ed.), *The Security of Oceania in the 1990s* (Canberra: Strategic and Defense Studies Center, Research School of Pacific Studies, Australian National University, 1990), p. 47.
29.   Joint Committee, p. 49.
30.   Quoted in ibid.
31.   Muriel Brookfield and R. Gerard Ward, *New Directions in the South Pacific* (Canberra: Academy of the Social Sciences, Research School of Pacific Studies, Australian National University), p. 16.
32.   Joint Committee, p. 37.
33.   Jeremy Carew-Reid, *Environment, Aid, and Regionalism in the South Pacific* (Canberra: National Center for Development Studies, Australian National University, 1989), p. 118.
34.   Quoted in ibid., p. 129.
35.   Joint Committee, pp. 194–5.
36.   Gareth Evans, 'Alliances and Change', talk delivered at Edward Clark Center for Australian Studies, University of Texas, Austin, 9 October 1990.
37.   Michael Hammel-Green, *The South Pacific Nuclear-Free Zone Treaty* (Canberra: Peace Research Center, Research School of Pacific Studies, Australian National University, 1990), p. 65.
38.   Richard Bolt, 'The New Australian Militarism', in Graeme Cheeseman and St John Kettle (eds), *The New Australian Militarism* (Sydney: Pluto Press, 1990), p. 54.
39.   Gary Smith, 'Two Rhetorics of the Region', in Cheeseman and Kettle (eds), p. 122.

40. Joint Committee, p. 156.
41. Graeme Cheeseman, 'Overreach in Australia's Regional Military Policy', in Cheeseman and Kettle (eds), p. 81.
42. Joint Committee, p. 157.
43. Ewan Jamieson, *Friend or Ally: New Zealand at Odds With Its Past* (Sydney: Brassey's Australia, 1990), p. 3.
44. John Henderson, 'New Zealand's Non-Nuclear Regional Approach to Security', in Hegarty and Polomka (eds), p. 43.
45. David Hegarty and Peter Polomka, 'New Thinking on Security', in ibid., pp. 6–7.
46. Henderson, p. 63.

Chapter 9: Japan's New Regional Economy

1. Richard Cronin, *Japan's Expanding Role and Influence in the Asia-Pacific Region: Implications for US Interests and Policy* (Washington, DC: Congressional Research Service, 7 September 1990), p. 7.
2. Ibid., pp. 75–6.
3. Ibid., p. 9.
4. Ministry of Foreign Affairs, *Japan's Official Development Aid 1990 Annual Report* (Tokyo: Ministry of Foreign Affairs, 1991), p. 43.
5. K. Matsuura, 'Administering Foreign Aid: The View From the Top', *Economic Eye*, Spring 1989, pp. 12–13.
6. Dick Nanto, *Pacific Rim Economic Cooperation* (Washington, DC: Congressional Research Service, 3 April 1989), p. 10.
7. Saburo Okita, 'Asian-Pacific Prospects and Problems for the Further Development of the Asian-Pacific Cooperative Framework', paper presented at the Symposium 'In Search of a New Order in Asia', Santa Barbara, California, 1–3 February 1990, p. 2.
8. Nanto, p. 11.
9. 'Competition Worries Taiwanese Manufacturers', *Electronics Business*, 10 December 1986, p. 43.
10. Suh Ki-Sun, 'Failure to Restructure Industry at Root of Economic Woes', *Business Korea*, February 1991, p. 43.
11. Song Byung-Nak, 'The Korean Economy', unpublished manuscript, Seoul, 1989, p. 174.
12. Kang Duck-Joong, 'Structural Problems at Root of Illness', *Electronics Korea*, July 1990, p. 11.
13. Urban Lehner, 'Taiwan Worries its Reliance on Technology From Japan Could Hurt its Competitiveness', *Asian Wall Street Journal Weekly*, 8 July 1991, p. 18.
14. Jacob Schlesinger, 'Hitachi Joins Goldstar in Plan for Chip Plant', *Asian Wall Street Journal Weekly*, 31 July 1989, p. 6.
15. Konomi Tomisawa, 'Development of Future Outlook for an International Division of Labor in the Automobile Industries of the Asian NICs', briefing paper for First Policy Forum of the International Motor Vehicle Program, Cambridge, Massachusetts, 5 May 1987, p. 17.
16. Ibid., p. 68.

17. Ibid.
18. Ibid., p. 34.
19. Werner International, 'Spinning and Weaving Labor Cost Comparisons', New York, Spring 1989.
20. 'Government Eager to Cut Deficit', *Korea Times*, 12 January 1992; reproduced in *Foreign Broadcast Information Service*, 14 January 1992, p. 32.
21. '"Silver Lining" Seen in Asian Investment Cut', Survey, *Australian Financial Review*, 28 October, p. 53.
22. James Clad, 'Investment Flows Into and Out of Korea', *Korea Economic Update*, Vol. 2, No. 2 (Summer 1991), p. 1.
23. James MacGregor, 'Taiwan Firms Head Overseas as Costs Increase at Home', *Asian Wall Street Journal Weekly*, 14 August 1989, p. 18.
24. Jeremy Mark, 'Taiwanese Trade Surplus Rose in 1991 on Ties to Mainland and Southeast Asia', *Asian Wall Street Journal Weekly*, 13 January 1992, p. 15.
25. Rob Steven, *Japan's New Imperialism* (Armonk, New York: M.E. Sharpe, 1990), p. 170.
26. Ibid., p. 116.
27. Nanto, p. 11.
28. Alan Rix, *Japan's Aid Program: A New Global Agenda* (Canberra: Australian International Development Assistance Bureau, April 1990), p. 40.
29. David Arase, quoted in ibid., p. 39.
30. 'Thailand', Survey, *Financial Times*, 3 December 1991, p. 15.
31. Suthy Prasartset, *Democratic Alternatives to Maldevelopment* (Yokohama: International Peace Research Institute Meigaku [Prime], 1991), pp. 2–3.
32. Steven Schlosstein, *Asia's New Little Dragons* (Chicago: Contemporary Books, 1991), p. 163.
33. Ibid., p. 164.
34. 'Delta Force', *Far Eastern Economic Review*, 16 May 1991, p. 67.
35. James MacGregor, p. 20.
36. James Elliott, 'Natural Magnet for Taiwan', Survey, *Financial Times*, 24 April 1991, p. v.
37. 'Delta Force', p. 67.
38. 'Source Says Banks to Open Offices in Vietnam', *Tokyo Shimbun*, 11 February 1992; reproduced in *Foreign Broadcast Information Service*, 13 February 1992, Annex 1.
39. 'Low-cost Yet Capable Labor Force Among Vietnam's Big Attractions', *Nikkei Weekly,* 22 June 1991, p. 17.
40. Quoted in Victor Mallet and Peter Ungphakorn, 'We Can Move Up the Ladder', interview with Prime Minister Anand Panyarachun, Survey, *Financial Times,* 3 December 1991, p. 17.
41. Victor Mallet, 'The Focus Switches to Technology', Survey, *Financial Times*, 3 December 1991, p. 17.
42. Ross Garnaut, *Australia and the Northeast Asian Ascendancy* (Canberra: Australian Government Publishing Service, 1989), p. 1.
43. Geoff Brennan, 'Australia No Longer Just a Quarry for Raw Materials', Survey, *Australian Financial Review*, 28 October 1991, p. 77.

44. Steve Burrell, 'Investment Explosion, But the Direction Changes Dramatically', Survey, *Australian Financial Review*, 28 October 1991, p. 44.
45. Quoted in Abe David and Ted Wheelwright, *The Third Wave: Australia and Asian Capitalism* (Sydney: Left Book Club Cooperative, 1989), p. 34.
46. Australian Manufacturing Council, *The Global Challenge: Australian Manufacturing in the 1990s* (Sydney: Australian Manufacturing Council, 1990), p. 8.
47. Ibid., p. 18.
48. As described by David and Wheelwright, p. 50.
49. Garnaut, p. 220.
50. Quoted anonymously in Michael Wines, 'Australia's Focus, like Bush's, is Tokyo', *New York Times*, 3 January 1992, p. A3.

Chapter 10: The US–Japan Relationship

1. 'Review of Current Trends: US Foreign Policy', Policy Planning Staff Paper 21, in Thomas Etzold and John Lewis Gaddis (eds), *Containment: Documents on American Policy and Strategy, 1949–50* (New York: Columbia University Press, 1978), p. 228.
2. Donald Gregg, 'Korea: A War Worth Fighting For; A Relationship Worth Preserving', *Korea's Economy*, Vol. 7, No. 1 (1991), p. 14.
3. Takafusa Nakamura, *The Postwar Japanese Economy: Its Development and Structure* (Tokyo: University of Tokoyo Press, 1980), pp. 41–2.
4. This attitude was expressed by Navy Secretary John Lehman when he told Congress, 'We consider the Philippine bases critical to our strategy in the Pacific and Indian Ocean. We do not plan to leave.' 'National Security Interests in the Philippines', Testimony presented at hearing of US Senate Armed Services Committee, Subcommittee on Military Construction, 10 April 1986, p. 4. The Navy eventually had to leave, courtesy of the Philippine Senate, but not before it had put up a tremendous fight to stay in Subic.
5. Richard Solomon, assistant secretary of state, Statement before the US House of Representatives Foreign Affairs Committee, Subcommittee on East Asian and Pacific Affairs, 6 March 1991, p. 9.
6. Quoted in *The Economist*, 18 May 1991, p. 52; and *New York Times*, 20 June 1991, p. 3.
7. Andrew Dougherty, 'Japan 2000', New York, Rochester Institute of Technology, 11 February 1991, p. 79.
8. Ibid., p. 35.
9. Ibid., p. 167.
10. Ibid., p. 158.
11. Quoted in 'Beneath Talk of New Partnership with US, Serious Tensions Grow', *Los Angeles Times*, 11 December 1990, p. H3.
12. Ibid.
13. Steven Vogel, *Japanese High Technology, Politics, and Power* (Berkeley, California: Berkeley Roundtable on the International Economy, March 1989), pp. 98–9.

14.   *Los Angeles Times*, 11 December 1990, p. H3.
15.   Ibid.

Chapter 11: Towards a New Order in the Pacific
1.   Donald Gregg, Speech before Asia Society, New York, 30 November 1990.
2.   Barbara Crosette, 'US Aide Calls Muslim Militants Concern to World', *New York Times*, 1 January 1992, p. 3.
3.   Gareth Evans, 'Alliance and Change', Speech delivered at the University of Texas, Austin, 9 October 1990.
4.   'Hands on Asia', *The Economist*, 16 November 1991, p. 17.
5.   Joseph Camilleri, 'New Approaches to Regional Security', unpublished paper, Melbourne, 1991.
6.   *Asahi Evening News*, January 1990.

Index